The Jacques Romano Story

THE
JACQUES ROMANO
STORY

by Berthold Eric Schwarz, M.D.

University Books Inc. • New York

In Memory of Eric

CONTENTS

CONTENTS

PREFACE

Jacques Romano's life has great meaning for anyone who is interested in living long and staying young, in developing self-awareness and psychic abilities. He was an inspiring example of what can be done. It is my purpose to present this extraordinary man in sharpest focus, largely using his own words. What he said and what he did speak for themselves.

It was my privilege to know and study Jacques Romano from age ninety-two to his death at ninety-eight. I promised him that I would prepare a manuscript about him. After many years and revisions I have put together as factual and complete a picture of him as seems possible.

To his many friends and other good people who knew Jacques Romano and who assisted me in this study I extend heartfelt thanks. By searching their memories and records they performed a labor of love and, it is hoped, left a fitting memorial to a dynamic man who in his long lifetime was energy personified.

Particular thanks go to the eminent researcher and internist, Dr. Seymour S. Wanderman, who was Jacques and Molly Romano's personal physician for more than

forty years. I am also grateful to my colleague and friend,
Dr. Bartholomew A. Ruggieri, for his careful reading and
constructive, scientific criticism of the study. My apprecia-
tion goes to Mrs. Isabelle M. Sayre, who typed the original
research protocols and manuscripts many times over, and
more recently my personal secretary, Miss Vilma Semsey,
and my manuscript typist, Mrs. Virginia Stevens. In her
editing, Mrs. Joan W. Jesurun has demonstrated her skill
with the English language.

The quotations under the chapter headings are mainly
Jacques Romano's own words.

I take full responsibility for any errors, which are completely unintentional.

I

JACQUES ROMANO'S PRESCRIPTION FOR SELF-MASTERY

"Jacques is about eleven shades different from anybody you have ever met before."

—RIAN JAMES, 1931, IN "REVERTING TO TYPE"

"THE grand ballroom of the Waldorf Astoria was packed. The Prince of Wales was delivering the main speech. He had the audience in the palm of his hand. A door opened in the back of the room and a wiry little man quietly entered and took a seat in an obscure corner. The Prince of Wales stopped short, looked at the dapper, vivacious man in the black suit and bow tie, gave a snappy military salute, bowed, and said, 'Jacques Romano, how good to see you!' "

This vignette typifies Romano and his place in the society of his day—but he did not tell it. In fact, this anecdote comes from the Reverend Dr. Howard Mac-Donald, who had known Romano for many years, and who during Romano's funeral rose to say a few words. Romano never made any claims but left it to others to recall his spectacular feats and amazing comments.

Like Jacques's friends in life, all of us at the funeral were in agreement that he was the most unusual, completely extraordinary, and amazingly interesting man we had ever met. His character and abilities were incomparable and he was incorruptible.

Many of us at the funeral recalled our own favorite experiences and stories about this fabulous man who in almost a century of life had traveled the world over, loved, painted, invented, performed extraordinary healings, convulsed people with his witty stories, and opened their hearts to truth and self-awareness.

For example, although badly in need of money for his own requirements, he preferred to keep his promise and speak to some young people at a certain church gathering than to go to an exclusive hotel to meet fifteen or twenty people and receive five hundred dollars for a few hours' visit. His unique talents were never for sale.

Mystic or magician, holy man or iconoclast? Psychic, after-dinner speaker, entertainer, pioneer aviator, chemist, salesman, and soldier of fortune—all describe the spry, sharp-witted, little ninety-eight-year-old New Yorker whose vigor and appearance bore witness to his discovery of the fabled fountain of youth.

Jacques Romano, according to his close friend and personal physician of more than forty years, Dr. Seymour S. Wanderman of New York, had almost limitless opportunities for personal aggrandizement, for power politicking, and even for meddling in international affairs. Yet he never made any effort to capitalize on his abilities for financial gain or personal power. Neither did he descend to manipulation of other people's affairs—whether they were highly placed or not. Many documented instances reveal that Romano could tune in on people, know their secret thoughts, loves, and pains. He could even foretell the future.

At his simple funeral service it was evident how

Jacques's friends treasured all the experiences, points of view, and secrets he had shared with them from his long and active life. This was the man who in his nineties looked thirty years younger and who had more bounce, sparkle, and wit than many just entering the prime of life. Jacques Romano was a human dynamo almost to the very end. By his example he showed what a human being is capable of: how to live long and drink to the very end the full measure of the sweetness and vibrancy of life, how to be a joy to others and to be sought out. Romano had a message to make people pay attention and listen as they never did before in their lives. His accomplishments and what he could demonstrate before their eyes were sufficient proof of his willingness to open his heart and mind and reveal treasured secrets to those who wished to learn.

As I sat through the funeral service, pictures and memories flashed through my mind. There was the recent grim experience of pronouncing my friend dead. Having witnessed so many strange things Romano had done in the past, I specifically noted his stopped watch before entering the bedroom for the examination necessary for filling out the death certificate. Upon my return to the living room I was shocked to see that his watch had spontaneously started running again. When the others in the room, who were far removed from the watch, were questioned about this, they were also very surprised. No one had been near the watch and there was nothing to account for its running again.

There was the jolly, typically ridiculous situation of a few years ago, when during a Romano party Jacques gave a very dignified, elderly society lady thirteen cards from a deck. Romano fanned the deck out in the lady's hands and then looked at the cards for a few seconds. He returned them to the lady's view and proceeded to call them out.

Finally, with only three cards left, he asked, "Have you the two of diamonds?"

The society lady said, "No. I do not."

Romano said, "I'll bet you a nickel you have the two of diamonds."

"No!"

Romano and the lady seesawed back and forth. He insisted and she denied. She became increasingly indignant. Romano's eyes twinkled and she flushed and turned crimson. The audience exploded with amusement and applause.

"You're right! I've got the two of diamonds. I think you did something to that two of diamonds!" The embarrassed society matron had just been mentally released by the "tottering nonagenarian"! For the first time she recognized the card in front of her eyes which he was calling out.

Romano didn't particularly care who people were, and he was at home in almost every situation. He told this incident of long ago:

"I was in a Georgia hotel showing some fellows card tricks. Another man was sitting in the lobby, so I asked him to please take a card. He looked up and said, 'I don't know one card from another.' I nodded my head, and the other fellows said that this man was a reverend. The minister then said, 'You would also be better off if you did not know one card from the other.' I answered: 'If you don't know one card from the other, that is your business, but to advise me is reprehensible. Now, Reverend, let us compare ourselves. You don't play cards because you don't know one card from another. And I know cards and every crooked game from every place on the face of the earth, and I don't play cards. Now, who is the better man, you or

I? You don't play because you don't know how to play, and I merely do not choose to play. So who has more character? You or I?' "

*   *   *

It was a cold, bleak December day, in 1955, when I met Jacques Romano. I had gone into New York City to meet this man of whom I had heard so much. But I had dismissed most of it as either idle talk or the fantastic fabrications and gullibility of my Dartmouth College classmate, Dr. Roy Swenson. Surely Roy must have been hoaxed or deluded. However, he made Romano appear interesting.

That meeting in Romano's drafty Maiden Lane laboratory changed my life. Although I had been a doubter, my hard-nosed skepticism and scientific distrust were gradually changed over a six-year period of studying Jacques Romano under all conceivable conditions and even living with him.

Much of the material about Romano has had to be painstakingly pieced together from crumbling newspaper clippings, old photographs, odd memorabilia, and some personal correspondence with surviving friends. Fortunately, the subject of the study, Jacques himself, was very much alive; in fact, he appeared to be twenty-five to thirty years younger than his stated age when we first met.

He was thin, trim, and self-confident. He had wavy graying hair, penetrating but kind dark eyes. He spoke in a crisp voice and moved from subject to subject with ease. He added a dash of humor to his comments.

It was possible for me to spend several hundred hours with Romano and conduct a frank, firsthand study without restrictions, taboos, or any strings attached, save one: to report what was observed in as factual and straightforward a manner as possible.

In his long and exciting career Romano had been known (and yet unknown) throughout the world for his feats. Although he would not call himself a "psychic," or a "medium," or use any abracadabra or mystical language, he was an enigma whose story was still unfolding. Oddly enough, he was a man who raced through life so furiously that his experiences had never been fully recorded.

For example, Rian James wrote in his column "Reverting to Type," in 1931: "He [Romano] meets about two hundred new people each day; refuses to bother with names; will, when a name is actually pushed on him, read it backwards to see if it has any significance when unrolled that way; and will, also, when you demand, plead for, and actually beg an appointment with him, pull out a worn little black book, and note the appointment in it. He generally makes his appointments about seven weeks in advance, immediately forgetting forevermore that any appointment has been made."

The material about Romano has been checked and rechecked from tape recordings we made together. Romano's descriptions of events in his past life seldom, if ever, showed discrepancies in essential details from the reports given by his friends.

Unfortunately it was impossible to verify many interesting situations in his long life. This process of piecing together various items and data is analogous to the joys, challenges, and frustrations of an archeologist when uncovering some priceless, ancient *objet d'art* and trying to rejoin the crumbled fragments as perfectly as possible. This problem is not unique; for the physician, in the course of a complete examination, must listen carefully to his patient's story, observing how his patient tells his story and how he reacts. This practice, when combined with a careful physical examination, and at times special laboratory tests, provides a basis for the physician's evaluation and offer of help.

Because of so many presumed psychic experiences in Romano's life, it is regrettable that in some instances more complete information is not obtainable. Nevertheless, Romano's honesty, his many excellent character references, successful spot checks of data, and the absence of gross contradictions, plus the striking results obtained in many firsthand experiments, make it imperative that as much be recorded as possible.

Newspaper clippings dating back to near the turn of the century and personal interviews with some of his friends reveal that Romano was then doing many of the same spectacular and mysterious things he still was doing in his nineties.

Many of his friends, for example, recall how Romano had talked about longevity and health for close to fifty years. Early in life Romano set his sights on a goal of longevity, made known his purpose, and succeeded in reaching his goal. His accomplishment is unique. Here is a man who was his own prophet. Unlike many of us, he knew what he was talking about. He declared his mission in full view of the whole world. He not only succeeded— for nowadays to survive into advanced age is not as extraordinary a feat as fifty years ago—but he showed by example how a human being can be completely capable of an active, alert, creative, virile, and healthy life—not mere existence but life—well into the ninth decade—nearly the century mark!

What Romano had to say about longevity means much more than just living or existing. It means the joy and love of life with the throttle pulled out all the way. He was a man with a message for all who wish to share his secret of a long, healthy, active life.

Many others, including dietary faddists, self-styled swamis, and assorted fanatics, declared similar goals of longevity for themselves but failed to achieve them. Not a few celebrated physicians loudly proclaimed this quest for themselves and their patients. Yet, despite complex extracts of sex glands, courses of vitamins, serum injections, and delicate surgery, they not only failed to be rejuvenated but died long before reaching the proverbial three score and ten.

What sort of man was it who in his nineties still rose at five every morning, prepared his own breakfast, took a brisk walk to the subway and rode to his Jamol Company laboratory in downtown Manhattan, where he put in fifteen hours of work, inventing, manufacturing, packing and mailing an assortment of iodine-containing proprietary drugs? (Romano would often quip that upon entering his office he was the doorman. In the laboratory he was the chemist and, when sitting at his desk, the president. "When I find that the place needs sweeping out, I'm also the janitor. Then, when the place is all cleaned up, I elevate myself to president of the company again—unanimously.")

What was different about his outlook on life, his diet, dreams, exercise, and activities? How might his subconscious life have differed from that of others? And in what ways might these factors have influenced his long life, excellent health, and his apparent telepathic, clairvoyant, and prophetic-psychic experiences? What secrets might account for these accomplishments, and how did Romano explain the great degree of control he seemed to possess over so many diverse and strange abilities?

With his multifaceted personality, Romano was confidant, advisor, healer, and more, to politicians, royalty, rulers, clergymen, housewives, professional people, and men and women from all walks of life. Yet Romano cared not who people's ancestors were, but what they themselves were, how they behaved, and what they could do.

Some of Romano's anecdotes and experiences involved prominent people like Teddy Roosevelt, Enrico Caruso, Henry Ford, Thomas Edison, Madame Blavatsky, Lillian Russell, Mark Twain, and King George VI. Others who crossed his path included Sir Arthur Conan Doyle, Edgar Cayce, Josef Hofmann, William James, "Texas" Guinan, Alfred Adler, John Hays Hammond, Pope Pius XII, Al Smith, Arturo Toscanini, Mary Baker Eddy, Jules Bache, Charles Lindbergh, and a collection of savages, holy men, and just plain people. However, the listing of famous names and raking up of sometimes salty situations from the past are of little consequence in attempting to understand Romano. These people were in *Who's Who,* and he was not, but to him it made no difference. He was the center of the stage. He never sought them out. They sought him.

II

HOW TO GET THE MOST OUT OF LIFE

"I was born with a peculiar kink in the brain, and one would have to be either a genius or an imbecile to have such a kink."

J ACQUES Romano was born April 16, 1864—in "God's country," as he put it. He emphatically disavowed any nationality or culture, since "everyone's ancestors could only be proud of being pagans, cutthroats and thieves, who divided up God's world and then greedily fought over it." When asked about his family background, Romano would often become perturbed and say, "I do not want to talk of my family in any shape or form because I have not seen them in seventy years. I am an individual and never wanted to imitate anybody. Each brother and sister was born in a different country. There was a complete lack of routine.

"I was different from the others. I was born with a peculiar kink in the brain, and one would have to be either a genius or an imbecile to have such a kink. With my own particular way of thinking, I did not fit into the family scheme, and they called me *cabeza dura* (pigheaded) . I never told my parents but I used to wonder if I were an adopted child. No one understood me. I couldn't play a musical instrument, sing, recite, or memorize two lines. My teachers wanted me to memorize, but I couldn't. If my parents wanted to give me something, I would not let them."

Throughout the years Romano never changed his attitude toward his family. When asked about his parents or some of his early childhood experiences, he often smiled and replied, "I always pictured myself as coming from a good family and home. This made me feel that I was better than the type of people I met when I first landed in the United States in 1885.

"While in Europe, I heard a lot about Abraham Lincoln; that he was a man who had no social background or wealth and yet had become President of the United States. When I was in America for only a short time, I saw his picture and was fascinated by his face. I even wondered, 'How could such a homely man ever become the President of the United States? No one knew or cared who his parents were until he became the Great Lincoln.' This proved to me that if a person has the quality within himself he can always succeed without depending on social standing and wealth. From then on, I decided to discard all the grandeur instilled in me by my family. I decided to be myself, belonging to no country, and forever an orphan without family attachments. From that day until today, I have had no interest in, or any form of relationship to, my past life and family.

"My birthplace became God's world, and my home, by choice, became the United States. I looked upon the other countries and various forms of religions I encountered with tolerance and as a good neighbor. I am my own master and my own slave, and I work steadily, day by day, to live out these beliefs. The example of Abraham

Lincoln's life became an inspiration. Abraham Lincoln did more for me than my parents' wealth and position."

*   *   *

From the time he entered young manhood until his twenty-first year Jacques Romano traveled throughout Europe, Siberia, and Russia. It was during these trips that he acquired much of his storehouse of knowledge and his uncanny powers of observation. When he first came to the United States in 1885, he stayed only four months because "there were no soldiers and my sense of propriety was shocked at seeing a gentleman employer dressed in a high silk hat and Prince Albert coat having a drink in a saloon with a laborer. What kind of a country could this be?"

Upon returning to Europe, he traveled for another four years in exotic lands now familiar to him. In 1889, when twenty-five years old, Romano made a second trip to the United States. Shortly after arriving, he supported himself by working for Moreno and Lopez, New York photographers. He remembered photographing the Infanta Eulalia, and recalled how his mother's knowing Sarah Bernhardt got him a job with Napoleon Sarony for six-dollars-a-week wages! Later, he worked for Falk and other photographers. During these early years he became well acquainted with many of the celebrities he photographed: Madam Schumann-Heink, the de Reszkes, Emma Eames, Lillian Russell, Melba.

LEARNING ENGLISH

Romano once recalled an amusing incident of this time in his life. "When I had been in the United States only a short time, I really did not know much English. While working for Moreno and Lopez, the photographers, I hypnotized many of the Spanish and French-speaking people in the building. There was an Irishman, Mike, who swept the studio; he asked me to hypnotize him. I told him to look me in the eyes and sleep. After a short while, I said, 'Now Mike, finished; get up!' Mike got up. I was a little surprised and said, 'Sit down.' However, he got up again when I said, 'Get up.' It was a difficult situation because I did not know how to say 'Wake up.' I snapped my fingers hoping he would wake up, but instead he got up and started to climb the wall. In my exasperation I ran out into the street and found a friend to interpret for me so that I could finally wake up Mike. After that incident I made up my mind never to hypnotize until I knew how to speak English."

HOW TO SPEAK ANY LANGUAGE IN TWO WEEKS

Romano's unconventional method for learning a language was once reported in the newspapers.

"You need only 125 words to make yourself understood. For instance, some of the words are 'yes, no, here, there, over, under, bread, water, fire, pain, I have, I have not, I work, I work not.' The less vocabulary you have when you get mad, the more emphatically you employ emotion. If you learn ten essential words a day, in two weeks' time you will have the basic vocabulary. Practice by talking to yourself for two days until you finally try speaking to others. If then they don't understand you, it isn't my fault, because they did not learn their language by my method."

*   *   *

Romano's familiarity with many languages and different cultures and his occult powers gave him entree into both the melting-pot immigrant and old-line society of New York City. In the early 1890's he painted miniatures of New York society women for Peter Mallé, and in 1898 he was involved with the Cuban revolution. During the 1900 Buffalo Exposition (which was actually held in 1901) Romano was manager for the Eastman Kodak exhibit. He worked his way up, became one of their top salesmen, and was assigned to vast areas of the United States, Mexico, and South America. While engaged in his job of selling photographic equipment, he managed to become involved in various Latin American intrigues and adventures.

SOUTH OF THE BORDER

"In Latin America they had no soldiers; everyone was a colonel or a general. They bought their uniforms from Germany. Once the man who carried my baggage into the hotel was dressed like a field marshal.

"Having watched governments come and go in various Latin American blood baths, I concluded that when two people fight each other for a new form of liberty, it is really for a new form of slavery. These people spend their lives fighting their fellowmen, rather than developing the limitless natural resources of their countries."

HAITIAN KNIFE

"While traveling for Eastman Kodak I had to go to Haiti. The first stop was a small coastal town. At that time

Haiti was a primitive country, not unlike central Africa. I had to go to Port-au-Prince, so I bought a horse, a compass, and a map, and started out before sunup. As a precaution I had a long rope, one end of which was tied to the horse and the other end to my foot. The country was mountainous.

"During the second night of the trip, just before sunrise, I suddenly became restless and awakened. I stood up, bowed my head, and then saw a tall, muscular Negro standing over me. He said that he could kill me if he wanted to; he was intent on robbing me. He had a big revolver, but it was rusted and did not look too good. I thought he wanted to threaten me with it, but he suddenly pulled out a knife and said, 'Now I can kill you!'

"If I had given way to my fear, I might have dropped dead from heart failure—my brain would have been paralyzed. Ever since boyhood I had learned that fear is self-destructive, and so I became composed and retained control of my faculties.

"Then I noticed how the sun glittered on the knife's blade, and I said to the man, in his native tongue, 'What a beautiful knife, let me buy it from you. I'd like to have it to take to the United States as a souvenir. Are you sure you made it yourself? It is one of the most beautiful knives I have ever seen. You must sell it to me for my collection.' The native was astounded—thrown completely off balance. He looked at me dumbly, then admitted he had fashioned the knife. For the knife I gave him all the change in my pocket. He spent some time with me and showed me the road. Later when I told my story in Port-au-Prince, they said that under a new law this man could not have fired his pistol without the serious risk of being shot on the spot if caught. The native walked off with my change. I walked off with his knife and my life."

MAYAN RUINS

Today's archeologist might disagree with some of the opinions and conclusions in the following examples which afford a glimpse of Romano's personality and powers of observation. At the turn of the century much less was known about various ancient Indian civilizations than is known today.

"I had to go to Merida, the capital of Yucatan. There I saw two men who looked rather peeved and restless. I asked, 'What's the trouble?' They asked me if I spoke English and said that they had come to visit the ruins. They introduced themselves as Professor Hewett, American Archaeological Society, and Professor Smith of the Royal Archaeological Society. They had been in Merida several days but could not get permission to go to the ruins. I said, 'Gentlemen, I'll be glad to help you if you will take me to the Palace of the Governor.' So the three of us went to the Palace, where I spoke to the Lieutenant-Governor. My actions and manners were those of a Spanish nobleman. I told him I was a doctor and a writer on spiritualism. After hearing my story, the Lieutenant-Governor ushered me in to see the Governor, and I entered his office, a room about sixty feet long and forty feet wide, very imposing. When I was half-way into the room, I bowed and saluted the Governor, then went up close to him, saluted and bowed again. He beckoned to me to sit down. My actions appealed to him, and he must have thought I was a grandee.

"When the Governor asked what I was doing, I told him that I was a doctor and writer on spiritualism and that I was particularly interested in the old natives of Mexico who had many mysterious qualities. I was careful not to say 'Indians' because all the people, including the Governor, are part Indian and might be self-conscious about it. I then showed him the magic cigarette paper trick and let him feel my pulse beat strongly and then disappear. I told him something about his parents, which was true, and then, in a quiet way, about an ailment I could see in his eyes, something they all have in Latin countries. 'All right, I'll be glad to make arrangements for you,' he grunted. Then he nodded to the Lieutenant-Governor and told him to give permission for 'Doctor' Romano and his 'two assistants,' Professors Hewett and Smith, to start out for the Mayan ruins.

"Professor Hewett insisted I should accompany them, so the following day we took a narrow-gauge train to a village close to the ruins. There we were met by the *alcalde* (mayor), mestiza girls, and a hemp millionaire's wife. We had a magnificent dinner dance. They were honored to meet Dr. Romano and his two assistants who were professors. I remember our hostess' beautiful French furniture, chinaware, and silver. Not quite aware of Latin propriety, the professors told me to ask our gracious hostess where her husband was, but fortunately she did not understand English; so I observed proper etiquette and said instead, 'Madam, they liked the soup so much they are curious about the recipe.' I kept translating. 'We've never seen furniture so beautiful, and in such a wild country!'

"Early the next morning we met our guide, got our horses, and rode all day to the ruins. While I was riding and talking to Professor Smith, he told me the one purpose of the expedition was to find any link between the Mayan culture of Yucatan and other countries that indicated the early migrations.

"We arrived at dusk, and on the walls of the ruins I saw carvings of llamas and other animals from Peru. I called this to Professor Smith's attention and he shouted, 'Eureka!

You have discovered the missing link that shows the Mayans might have originally come from the south and migrated north.' For this contribution Professor Smith said he would give me credit in the Royal Archaeological Society."

PERILS OF A MAYAN TOMB

"I had just entered the interior of a ruined Mayan temple. It was completely empty and very dark. While proceeding most gingerly, I wondered why the wooden door did not decay. I thought to myself, 'These unusual people must have had some materials in which they soaked the beams.' While I was standing in the middle of the chamber, I suddenly noticed a hornet buzzing above me. *Caramba!* I had stirred up a hornet's nest! In the tropics these insects can be as poisonous as snakes. Before it was too late, I put my hands in my pockets and ran so fast that the wind ballooned out my loose-fitting Chinese silk shirt. The riding breeches and puttees protected the rest of me. Later that day, the overseer told me that I was lucky not to have been seriously bitten. The shirt, which had never fitted properly, and which I had thought of discarding, might have saved me from much grief."

MEXICAN TEMPEST

"In 1909 I was on the Pacific Coast of Mexico for the Kodak Company. I had just missed a passenger steamer and was forced to take a freighter that carried only two or three passengers. I got the best cabin. There was freight below, and the deck was covered with crates.

"The captain asked, 'Señor, what is your business?' I said, 'I'm a doctor and a spiritualist.' I thought I'd have some fun with him, so I told him we would have a very rough voyage and that there would be a storm at exactly 8:00 P.M. At the time the captain and I were talking, the ocean was as smooth as glass; however, a terrific storm developed at 8:00 P.M., and I had to strap myself in my berth. I could hardly get out of my cabin during the height of the storm because there were ropes tangled all over the deck. At one point, I looked into an adjacent room and saw a Mexican woman and her child praying on their knees. Later I received a note from the captain asking when the storm would be over. I answered, 'Come back in half an hour, and I'll tell you.' When he returned, I said, 'Four o'clock,' and the storm completely abated at that time. The furniture in the mess hall was broken up, and everything was washed out. These presentiments came easily, because I had no marital concerns, family obligations, or worries. My mind was clear, with no distraction other than the sky and the sea. When we landed, I congratulated the captain on his expert seamanship, and he said, 'I'll never forget you, and you'll never travel on any of my boats again!' "

OAXACA "SAINT"

"It was late in the afternoon in 1910, and I was in a village in Oaxaca. While I was walking through the streets, a woman shouted at me, 'Idolo! Idolo!'—'Did I want to buy an idol?' I took the idol, pretended to swallow him, and then produced him from under my coat. The woman screamed and called the other Indians— '*Hijo del diablo. Hijo del diablo* (Son of the devil. Son of the devil).' I said, 'No, I am a son of God like everyone else.'

"She must have been a very religious woman, because her home was filled with holy water and decorated with many statues. She called the other people of the village to show them how I could put my finger in a flame. I picked up a statue of St. Peter and presented the illusion of swallowing him and then pulled him from my overcoat sleeve.

"Then an Indian came in with crutches. I knew many of these people. Once they get sympathy, they will never give up their crutches. That's their philosophy, whether they are beggars in India, peons in Mexico, or so-called civilized men. So I said, 'I am now going to bless you all, and I wish you to kneel.' I started to chant in English, 'I'm having a wonderful time.' For all I know, they thought it was Latin. I looked at the man with the crutches and said, 'Why don't you kneel?' He said, '*Santo*, I am paralyzed.' I said, 'Look at me; stand still; drop the crutches; step forward three steps!' I raised my foot, stepped back three steps, and he followed me. Then I quickly made him walk back three more steps. You see, I had his brain confused; by my walking backward very quickly he had no time to think and he was 'cured.' Then he joined the rest of the people who were kneeling.

"Immediately, I was a saint. The man who had walked kissed my hand. Everyone touched my clothes. I finally left the village at 4:00 A.M. for the ruins in the quarries and came back before sunset. When I returned, about two

hundred people were following in carriages and wagons—
blind people, paralyzed people, and children. I made up
plenty of 'holy' water and traced the sign of the Cross to
symbolize the Father, the Son, and the Holy Ghost. I had
a little whisk broom which I waved while saying, '*Por
Dios; por Dios; Santa Maria; Santa Maria.* Tomorrow
you'll feel different!' Before the sun rose the next morning
I was out for Vera Cruz."

THE WILD WEST

In 1903, Romano was in Wagoner, Oklahoma (then
called Indian Territory), and had to go to Muskogee on
business for Eastman Kodak. However, he could not make
connections, so he asked one of the local people for as-
sistance.

"He was a heavyset man, and muttered, 'You can do it
this evening or tomorrow at eleven.' He was a typical
western half-breed of the Indian Territory. I said that we
did not understand each other and that I was talking of
Tuesday and he was talking of Thursday. He got mad because he felt I had insulted him, and he said, 'Try to help
a fellow, and he gets fresh!' At that point a traveling man
came in and said, 'What's wrong with this fellow who is
sulking?' I said, 'I don't know.' The half-breed then bel-
lowed, 'God damn it, you know!' He glowered, called me
various cuss words and raised his hand to hit me. I steeled
myself and said, 'You can say whatever you want, but don't
you dare raise a hand over me, don't you dare threaten me,
because you can't tell what might happen.' I intently gazed
at him with both my eyes. He slowly put his hand down.

Finally, I rented a team of horses and rode to another town where I could catch the stage for Muskogee.

"The next afternoon, when I was waiting for the stage in the one saloon in the town, this tough character appeared and lumbered over to me. I said, 'Hello, how are you?' He mumbled while looking at me intensely, 'Who are you? Who are you? Who are you? I can't sleep or eat. I've got you on my mind all the time, and I have to see you.' I knew he was still under my influence, so I bought him a drink, snapped my fingers, and told him he would be all right. Maybe he thought I was a revenue agent!"

PIONEER AVIATOR

"I never learned to ride a bicycle or drive an automobile. Yet I became a pioneer aviator and was one of the first to fly around the Statue of Liberty. I had befriended an American businessman, Geddes, in Mexico during an epidemic that followed an earthquake. In 1911, a few years later, he telephoned me and asked if I would like to become General Manager of the Bleriot Monoplane Company at Fort George, New York. Finding this to be an interesting challenge, I resigned my job at Eastman Kodak and proceeded to learn flying *in the New York subways* before undertaking the manufacture of the plane.

"The main problem in flying impressed me as being landing of the craft. The aviator had to know when to lift his machine as he approached the earth; if he could not master this he would crash. In order to learn how to judge correctly the perception of changing distances with movement, I practiced with a folded newspaper in my hands while standing in the first car of a subway train. When I saw the signal lights flash I pretended to be flying. Then, when the lights changed, before arriving at the station, I moved the simulated stick (the newspaper) in my hands just fast enough to coordinate the speed of the train and distance to the passenger platform. Finally, when I actually flew for the first time, the man sitting next to me could not understand how I could figure the distance and do so well without any previous experience. We used a French-made three-cylinder rotary engine. The airport was at Mineola, Long Island.

"Years later, my wife Molly and I were at a party. Mary Pickford was accompanied by an elderly French gentleman, Monsieur de Valliere. The Frenchman and I were alone and he matter-of-factly remarked, 'I think I'll fly to Buffalo tomorrow.' I told him that I used to fly a little. He looked up, 'Really?'

" 'I was manufacturing the Bleriot machine!' He said, 'Yes?' and I said, 'The two McCormick Brothers, Charley and Willy, Wall Street brokers, put up the money.'

"Monsieur de Valliere smiled, 'Of course, now I can place you.' He remembered meeting Geddes, the Mc-Cormick brothers, and myself years ago. He was the Frenchman who sold the rights of manufacturing the Bleriot to the McCormicks."

Years later, in 1954, Jacques Romano's good friends, Mr. and Mrs. Louis Zara of Philadelphia, were visiting Horace Ashton, United States Cultural Attache in Haiti. Ashton himself, then in his seventies, had a life packed with adventure and action.

When they were discussing remarkable people they knew, the conversation shifted to early flying. Ashton, interrupting, said that the most unusual man he ever knew

was in New York, but that was about fifty years ago and
this man couldn't possibly be alive. Both Ashton and the
Zaras at once recognized the hero of early flying, as well
as countless other episodes—Romano!

*　　*　　*

Contrary to usual policy, the Eastman Kodak Company
took Romano back in 1912, and he remained with the firm
until 1914. Then he worked for John Hays Hammond,
who had widespread engineering and oil exploration in-
terests. Romano's "duties" consisted principally of being
a bon vivant and "court jester." During the war in 1917–
1918, he was connected with League Island, Philadephia,
as instructor on X rays, under the supervision of Dr. Jack
Da Costa. While there, Romano developed a process for
taking direct X-ray photographs and designed a Japanese
photographic factory.

A superb practical chemist, Romano did research on
iodine for six years, and in 1928 organized the Iodine
Company. From 1932 until his death in 1962, he was the
originator, compounder, and manufacturer of a variety of
iodine-containing medicines. This business, his Jamol
Company ("Ja" for Jacques, "Mol" for his late wife Molly),
continues today under the direction of Dr. Louis Cart-
nick, a friend of many years and the one to whom the
formulas were entrusted.*

Throughout the intervening years, Romano lectured
to many clubs, universities, and scientific organizations
on his philosophy, physical health, perennial youth, and
occult powers. He crossed the ocean many times during

* Romano's products include J-R Liquidine, an iodine solution for
internal use; Roma Nol, for external use; and Monodine, for accessible
mucous membranes. In addition, there are his best-known product,
Ponaris oil, and also Bahim oil and Avatar, cosmetic oil.

this period, and in 1937 he was invited to the coronation of King George VI.

Some comments tending to show the kind of man he was can be found in various newspaper articles through the years. They hailed his unusual talents. It should be stressed that Romano enjoyed the interviews but did not care one way or the other for the articles. The numerous clippings (collected by his late wife Molly) were haphazardly heaped in a cigar box. Among unidentified newspaper clippings from 1913 and June 14, 1915, were these: ". . . held an informal reception at his studio in the Oakland Apartments, to which his friends were invited to meet Mr. Jacques Romano, traveler, aviator and past master of psychic phenomena. Mr. Romano gave a most interesting talk on therapeutics, proving beyond doubt the marvelous power of mind over matter. With Mr. Romano the study of psychology is a hobby, and in his case cannot be confounded with professionalism. In any case, he eliminates all trickery and proves his wonderful power to be based solely on mental telepathy. Mr. Romano is also an artist of no mean ability in freehand drawing, and his efforts were enthusiastically appreciated."

*　　*　　*

"One of the most talked-of men on the cruise was Jacques Romano, of Rochester, New York. Mr. Romano had made a study of the action of the human mind and its susceptibility to suggestion and will.

"He is able to control the flow of blood in his body by making the blood flow into or withdraw from his arms at will. He demonstrated his power over others by influencing a subject. Dr. J. B. Kennedy examined a man under the spell of Romano and declared that his pulse had stopped entirely. 'It is beyond me,' he said."

From another unidentified clipping which appeared to come from the early 1930's:

"The chemist (Romano) held his extended fingers within two to six inches of the palms of a number of people in the room and all admitted feeling something like a cool breeze on their flesh; only they expressed it in different ways. One said it felt like a 'baby electric fan.' Mr. Romano explained he frequently cured headaches by the laying on of his hands.

"He did some expert work with playing cards, such as naming the thirteen cards which a man in the audience dealt to himself as a bridge hand. He made only two errors in the reading and begged to be excused for making the mistakes."

DIPS INTO SPIRITUALISM

"Getting into the realm of spiritualism, he gave what he called a 'little demonstration.' A well-known citizen, at his direction, helped himself to a cigarette paper. The citizen wadded it up into a tiny ball and held it between his finger tips. Mr. Romano told him to think of somebody who was dead. Then the demonstrator slowly spelled out the name 'J-O-H-N,' and said, 'that is the first name of the one you are thinking about.' The 'sitter' replied that it was.

" 'There was something wrong with his hands,' Mr. Romano said.

" 'He had two deformed fingers,' the man replied beginning to look startled.

"Mr. Romano made several statements concerning events in the life of the dead man, and the astonished citizen admitted they were true. Then Romano made a crease in the little paper ball with his finger nail and ran a lead pencil along the crease. All this time the paper was in the sight of nearby watchers.

" 'Now open the paper,' he said.

"The citizen did so and his face was a picture, as he read the word 'John' written in lead pencil and exclaimed: 'It is my father's handwriting!'

" 'I won't attempt to explain it,' he said later to his friends, 'but it is my father's handwriting all right.' "

*   *   *

In his column "The Seven Million" L. L. Stevenson wrote in the *Detroit News* for October 13, 1931:

"Continuing with that evening with Jack Romano in Harold Sherman's apartment with Mr. and Mrs. Cameron Moffat and a Brooklyn attorney and Mr. and Mrs. Sherman present: when it comes to mind reading, mediums, psychics and such, I'll admit I'm skeptical. Perhaps all those years in newspaper work, in which so many fakers have been encountered, are to blame for that. But Romano makes no claims for any out of the ordinary powers. That which he does, uncanny as it may seem, he does naturally. All that he claims is that his life is undistorted and that he knows how to think. He learned to think by observing animals and insects. But when a man tells you that your wife wants to get rid of a certain piece of furniture and that that piece of furniture is a radio, it gives you pause.

It gives you the well-known pause particularly since not two hours before there had been a home argument over the radio set that has been standing in the dining room for many years.

"That of course is trivial. But when that same person speaks of a business matter that has occurred in the spring, a matter of which he could not have had any knowledge, and goes on with it to a conclusion, then there is a feeling that there are things that cannot be explained. There is that same feeling when a dead person is described and the cause of death given accurately and unerringly along with certain physical traits and the fact that the dead person had worn a Masonic apron. Then there seems to be something uncanny, something eerie, something that indeed cannot be explained. The fact that Romano does not exploit his ability makes it all the more convincing."

A similar note was struck during the convention of the American Gastroenterological Association in 1932. On the same program with Drs. Walter Alvarez, Walter Palmer, Burrill Crohn, Albert Snell, and other distinguished physicians, Jacques Romano gave the formal banquet address. The printed announcement stated:

"Dr. Jacques Romano is known as a naturalist and the 'lone explorer' of the desert lands. His knowledge is based on personal observations, and he will tell us of philosophy and mysticism as practiced in India, Mongolia and Egypt: The Conscious over the Sub-Conscious, and medicine as practiced in the days of the Pharaohs; Suggestion and Auto-Suggestion, with demonstrations that so-called psychic phenomena and miracles are based on natural law."

Great Britain's *Sunday Chronicle* headlined on page 1 Romano's visit to England in 1935 and 1936.

February 24, 1935:

THIS MAN KNOWS EVERYTHING
He Can Cure Your Headache—Reveal Your Past—
Stop His Own Pulse
SAYS HE WILL LIVE TO 120
Amazing Mystic's Secrets

"A little man with piercing eyes—a man, who though more than 70, has the physique of a comparative youngster of 30—told me last night that he knew the secret of being able to live to be 120 and still die 'young.' "

And on February 2, 1936:

MAN OF MAGIC CROSSES SEA
FOR CARD PARTY CASE
Tricks He Would Have Shown the Judge

"Dr. Jacques Romano, Yogi, Chemist, criminologist, expert card-manipulator, reached London yesterday, summoned over the Atlantic telephone by financier Keith Williams.

"Dr. Romano arrived one day too late; he was to have given evidence for Mr. Williams in the Sunderland House card party action, which Mr. Justice Finley stopped on Friday.

"Lifelong student of the gambler's psychology, Dr. Romano would have shown the Judge just how easily innocent baccarat players may be swindled."

*   *   *

On May 7, 1940, Jacques Romano lectured to New York's Thinkers' Club. The accompanying bulletin was like previous comments:

"We want you to meet the amazing Jacques Romano . . . perhaps you have heard him over the Columbia Network on the 'Strange As It Seems,' 'Hobby Lobby,' or 'Mysteries of Mind' programs.

"Jacques Romano is the most remarkable man we have ever met. His demonstrations of the powers of the mind over matter are startling. Appearing before scientific and medical bodies and the staffs of outstanding universities, he has proved to be a physical and mental enigma.

"He graphically illustrates his talk with mental and physical demonstrations that are outstanding.

"His mind is rich in the lore of ancient and modern wisdom, and he gives you the knowledge of mental domination which you can apply in your daily life with telling effect, both physically and mentally.

"Although he insists there are no supernatural phenomena, his telepathic powers are uncanny, and through thought concentration he has full control of stopping the pulse beats, stopping the blood circulation, raising and lowering the blood pressure, stopping and starting the digestion.

"Jacques Romano has muscles of steel and the physical body of a young man. Yet he does not believe in so-called physical culture and goes through no ordinary physical exercises. We defy you to guess within 25 years of his actual age, which he will disclose at our meeting.

"At our last meeting one member who had heard Romano speak in London stated that he would not take $100 for the secret of health that he learned from Romano's talk. He said further that it would be difficult to place a true value on the information about Mental Mastery that Romano had given him."

Writing in the *New York Post* about a party of hers at the Waldorf Towers on October 10, 1942, Elsa Maxwell noted:

"The evening was a battle of magic between Orson Welles and a gentleman called Jacques Romano, who looks forty but admits to being seventy-nine. He is what one would call, I suppose, in Indian parlance, a Yogi—only he tells me that there are no Yogis nor has there ever been a Yogi in America.

"He read our minds 'as through a glass lightly.' I tried hard to think amiable, vacuous nothings for fear he would rout out my secret heart and give my particular show away. Cole Porter was terrified of Dr. Romano. Grace Moore loved being told about herself, as if she didn't know it already. Ania Dorfman, our greatest woman pianist, was thrilled and afterward played Liszt like mad and more brilliantly than anyone I have heard in many a day.

"Monty Woolley muttered sarcastic asides, and I got my biggest thrill when this seventy-nine-year-old miracle man, who claims he has discovered the philosopher's stone and learned the secret of eternal youth, asked me to feel his pulse. At the moment when it was beating strongest he calmly made it stop and suddenly Dr. Romano had no pulse at all. He told Neysa McMein, who was gazing up at him, fascinated, like a rabbit gazes at a snake, to hold out her hand. 'Now I will project ether through the ends of my fingertips on to the palm of your hand.' Neysa turned white and snatched her hand away, as she felt a cool breeze emanate from the Doctor's fingertips."

Finally here is a much more recent announcement printed by the New York Psychology Forum for a lecture on January 13, 1959:

"Jacques Romano—that incredible, amazing man. Here is a man who demonstrates the factors that metaphysicians, for the most part, talk about theoretically. At 95 he is still youthful, able to work fifteen or more hours a day with tremendous enthusiasm; who enjoys life to the fullest. What is his secret?

"He has learned much of the esoteric life—self-discipline, self-control and self-mastery from the Essenes. He learned how the mental can take care of the physical—for health and for patience—the spark of infinite time.

"Application of long-continued study, exhaustive, relentless self-training of the most rigid and unyielding nature have evolved a man who has developed his natural faculties to a degree unrecorded and unequaled in annals of modern science and medicine.

"No physical culturist, his body is that of a lean, lithe man half his years. His perceptions baffle and amaze his associates. He preaches no doctrine, espouses no faith, seeks no converts.

"An outstanding example of health, he believes that the normal span of life should not be less than 120 years. He describes how youthfulness, mental/physical activity may be maintained by exploiting the underdeveloped sources of vibrant energy latent in all of us."

III

LIVE LONG AND DIE "YOUNG"

"A doctor's wife cannot be treated by her husband because she knows all his failures and has no confidence in his treatment."

ROMANO'S philosophy of health and longevity was derived from observation of himself, his fellows, and animals in their natural habitats.* He carefully studied cause-and-effect relationships. "When I feel sick, I mentally go through everything that has happened to me for the past day. When I discover why I became sick, I try to correct the difficulty, and then I get better. When exposed to similar conditions in the future I handle myself differently by remembering the previous discomfort."

By carefully analyzing his feelings and bodily reactions in relation to nature and his social environment, Romano might have learned cause-and-effect relationships that are not apparent to most people. In this way he could have controlled anxiety and tension at their source, or at least turned them to constructive use.

Although not a Yogi, vegetarian, cultist, or devotee of any particular ritual, Romano followed certain self-imposed rules he learned from worldwide observations and

* As far as could be learned, there was no family history of longevity.

life experiences. His approach to life situations revealed the key to his problem: a realistic self-appraisal of his own psychic and physical capacities. He was careful not to exceed the limits of his endurance; yet, true to his nature of being different, he respected his own inclinations and habits without worrying about what the authorities might have to say.

His rule for exercise was simply, "Never exercise! The only sensible exercise I have found among American people is when they stand up and stretch at the seventh inning of a ball game. That is all right. The rest is not. Does an animal exercise? Did you ever see a sow doing sit-ups? The alligator does not exercise, breathes seldom, yet lives a hundred years. A turtle hardly moves, and lives to be a hundred. A dog races around all the time with his tongue out and is dead at fourteen. A rabbit takes seventy-five breaths a minute and lives eight years. A housefly goes zzz-zzz-zzz and drops dead in the soup! The fewer breaths a man takes the longer he can live. With practice I learned to get along on eight breaths a minute.

"There is also a relationship between breathing and the age of fertility. All creatures were intended to live twelve times as long as it takes a female to reach fertility, and this makes a man live, at least, 150 years. It works with animals. It should work with man."

Following his own rule, Romano's only formal exercise was what he had to do in his daily activities. He would often rather run up twenty flights of stairs than take an elevator. When he felt like it, Romano played kick ball with the children on the lawn in his ninety-fifth year, or he took a rather long walk in the country. On his ninety-eighth birthday he ran to catch a departing train in Pennsylvania Station in Newark, New Jersey. On one occasion he showed how he could toss eggs high up in the air and have them land on the lawn unbroken. Several weeks later the children tried to duplicate this feat to the amusement of passers-by, and their mother was shocked when she found a dozen eggs splattered on the front lawn.

Otherwise, Romano limited his exercise to "stretching out like a cat and then flexing [his] legs on [his] chest, upon awakening in the morning." Rather than sit in a soft, upholstered, easy chair, Romano often crouched down on his haunches. He reasoned that anything that grows is always in an oval and never a square. "It is a law of nature. The animal has three positions: squatting, lying down, and standing erect. Elephants go down on their knees, and most animals stretch out on their forelegs. Human beings, chimpanzees, and all bipeds sit on their haunches and assume a fetal position. The Japanese sit on their heels. When the Buddhists squat, they assume a religious symbol, with their legs and forearms flexed and their hands posed in a point. This makes a triangle which represents the physical, mental, and spiritual aspects. When a European sits in a chair, he denies the natural law of flexibility as seen when sitting on one's haunches. By sitting in a chair Western man assumes a square; then as he grows older he loses the flexibility of the legs and develops a cramped, unnatural posture, which contributes to many disabilities. In contrast, the Chinaman, who sits on his haunches for two or more hours, can then jump up quickly and run with his rickshaw. He maintains his flexibility into advanced age."

Superficially considered, an average of four to five hours of sleep a night would seem insufficient for health and contentment in most people. This brief rest can be sufficient, however, when supplemented by the unusual ability of a man like Romano to catnap at will for short periods of time during the day. Carefully performed experiments with Romano will be mentioned later (Chapter 8) that confirm this assertion and indicate that he utilized these brief catnaps of relatively deep physiological sleep to replenish his energy reserves.

He followed a pattern of sleeping in a uniform posture. He lay on his side, putting his hands up behind his head, like a monkey in the jungle. The apparent effectiveness of such a sleep pattern is further shown by the fact that, to the dismay of his fatigued host, Romano would often entertain from 7:30 on a Saturday night until 1:00 to 3:30 Sunday; then, after a short sleep, he would arise promptly at 6:30, push the heavy furniture back into position, and take a brisk stroll. Others might appear worn and half asleep, but Romano was bounding and chirping, as though nothing had happened the night before! He repeated this practice several nights a week throughout his life.

In order to maintain his health and minimize any abuse to his heart, Romano never overate. "I avoid foods that are hard to digest, and I never take anything into my stomach that I cannot put in my eye. I also never go to bed with cold feet. Many people die in their sleep because the heart must work much harder to keep their feet warm. The human being has proportionately larger legs than any other animal; and if he goes to bed with cold feet and legs, extra work must be done by the heart and that leaves him tired in the morning."

*   *   *

"The lion is strong because it eats nothing but meat. The horse is strong because it lives on a purely vegetable diet—and man is not because, like a hog, he will eat anything. . . . Milk is a much overrated food. Of course all animals understand the value of milk for their young. So have the oldest aborigines known the value of milk only for babies. How strange that chickens make so much calcium per day without drinking milk! Maybe the chickens suffer from miracles."

Many years ago Romano described his dietary habits in a memorandum he distributed with his line of Jamol Company drugs and cosmetics, to encourage others to achieve good health:

"The R-Menu tends to relieve the ill effects of congestion and to promote recovery from various ailments by keeping the body in a healthy condition.

"On arising, scrape the tongue with a teaspoon, removing the accumulated coating. Rinse the mouth and brush the teeth with your favorite toothpowder. Do not overeat at any one meal. Do not eat when tired, angry or worried. Take tea or coffee, nature's temporary substitute for food, till you can eat in peace.

"*MORNING* – an exclusively fruit meal. Grapefruit or orange juice diluted with an equal quantity of water from 1 to 3 glassfuls. The following variety of fruits may be taken: Grapes, apples, apricots, prunes, tomatoes, figs, bananas, dates.

"*NOON* – any kind of vegetables boiled or raw, vegetable soup, potatoes baked or boiled, corn or rye bread, cream cheese, bananas, dates.

"*EVENING* – any kind of vegetables, boiled and raw, any kind of fruit, meat, eggs or fish (always use lemon juice with fish). Nuts are a good substitute for meats. Do not eat fried food. Do not use table salt or condiments. You may use coffee or tea if desired—they are best taken one-half hour after meals."

Some of Romano's other dietary maxims are:

"1. To appease false hunger between meals take tomato juice, diluted with an equal quantity of evaporated milk.

"2. Children who are unduly excitable should not be overfed at any one meal, and should generally abstain from any rich foods, like eggs, cake, cocoa and chocolate in any form. In feeding children remember that they are often smarter than their parents. You never saw a tiger give one of its cubs a nickel to make it eat more, did you?

"3. The combination of bananas, dates, figs and cottage cheese with evaporated milk will be found healthful, nutritious and filling.

"4. Eat freely of lean meats, any kind of fruit, non-starchy vegetables. Do not resort to stimulants to overcome fatigue. Follow Nature's own remedy—sleep and rest.

"5. The R-Menu is not a diet—it is within the limit of compatible foods, avoiding unnatural stress to the body. Don't feed fried oysters to your horse for breakfast and don't eat them yourself. Although they are quite rich in minerals and vitamins, who wants to eat worms?

"6. It does not require medical assurance that when in good health one can eat anything and everything until sick from eating "Soup to Nuts"—then the all-devouring brave seek recourse in unpardonable coal-tar drugs, patent medicines and magic diets.

"7. Carbohydrate is a name given to sugars and starches which lend themselves to the manufacture of alcoholic beverages. However, the stomach does not recognize technical terms for the benefit of the brewing industry. A stomach may digest a potato and pass on its nutrition to the body, but the same stomach may revolt against starch in the form of bread. Always listen to your stomach and interpret its grumbling."

*   *   *

Romano extended moderation in foods to the use of drugs, tobacco, and alcohol. The only drug he took consistently through the years was his Jamol Company's iodine preparation, Liquidine. This is a 1 per cent aqueous solution of iodine and iodides. He took fifteen drops of this twice a day for forty years. Between thirty-four and fifty years of age, while working as a traveling salesman, Romano smoked only occasional cigars. He never inhaled. His alcoholic consumption consisted of a rare tablespoon of Bourbon whiskey in a glass of water at room temperature: "The Romano." However, if the occasion called for it, he would take a glass of beer or a cocktail.

"I could not understand how an educated man could become an alcoholic and a bum, so I left my fine clothes at the landlady's and became a tramp for six weeks. I hung out at Park Row in the Bowery, at a place called the Atlantic Garden. There I met a Bowery bum who was a Yale graduate and who often recited Shakespeare, Horace, and others for a nickel beer. Through him I met an English nobleman who was also a tramp. They had both been disappointed in love. The Englishman received two to three pounds a month. To show how he was raised and indoctrinated, he could never wash his face with water unless there was perfume in it. He was a highly educated man, very sensitive, and almost delicate. I remember one cold night he took his coat off and gave it to another tramp. After being so exposed he died a short time afterward of pneumonia. From these and other experiences I learned that most confirmed drunkards are gentlemen. They step aside and do not argue."

*   *   *

All aspects of bodily function were important to Romano. He understood how vital a healthy emotional outlook was, and the attention he gave to dietary habits was almost matched by his concern with elimination. He was careful to avoid any activities that might detract from his overall sense of well-being. He had learned how to remedy constipation by natural dietary means. Occasionally, when necessary, he managed his constipation with gentle tap water enemas. He also respected his urinary excretory needs. Although the prostate gland enlarged with advancing years (see Chapter 8) and complicated urination, he minimized undue stress on the bladder by resorting to frequent evacuation, sometimes using supplementary manual pressure on the abdominal wall directly over the bladder. He had some original views on this function. They were epitomized in his speculative comments on why only half as many women as men have rectal cancer.

"To urinate a woman simply sits down and is then able to more completely evacuate her bladder. A man urinates standing up, often in a hurry, and does not expel all the urine. As he gets older his prostate enlarges and aggravates this incomplete evacuation by anatomically obstructing the passage of urine. For these two reasons there is pressure on the front (anterior) of the rectum, and constipation results since bowel elimination is incomplete. The feces dry out and become like pebbles which scratch and irritate the lining of the rectum. This may be one factor accounting for the higher incidence of rectal cancer in men."

*   *   *

Dentists and people with dentures may be interested in Romano's unorthodox dental experiment.

"One evening (1934) at a dental meeting to which I had been invited, I was asked if I had ever given any thought to the subject of lower dentures which would fit so perfectly that mastication would not tend to loosen them, but would make them fit more securely. Scores of people had told me how they were embarrassed by the bottom set of false teeth becoming dislodged while eating. I began to consider how we eat. For instance, all animals with a short nose bite their meat off without effort, but an animal with a long jaw will bite, pull, twist, and turn to tear off meat. Since the crocodile cannot bite off a chunk of meat, he clamps his jaws on it and tries to tear the meat out. When he does not succeed he breaks it off by twisting. I thought of how we eat a banana. A banana is crushed by the tongue against the palate.

"Upon thinking over these examples and studying my own mastication, I found that one can bite off anything but can only chew by using the bicuspids and one molar on each side of the mouth. The dentists told me that the molars (the back teeth) were always less worn than other teeth. Man, I concluded, has inherited molars, which like his appendix he can well do without. To test this theory, which was opposed to dental procedure, I had all my good teeth extracted. My philosophy was that some day I would lose them anyhow, so I might as well benefit now. I told the dentist merely to dip a cotton pledget in water and apply it to the gums for local anesthesia.

"In all, I had six sets of false teeth made with slight variations by famous dentists, and yet not one of the lower plates gave satisfaction. I had to give up eating my accustomed foods. Finally, I took a chisel and file and removed the molars entirely from one of my sets—and found immediate comfort. Then I went to the University of Pennsylvania and laid my theories and my dentures before Dr. E. W. Smith, a celebrated dental surgeon. The Evans Institute of the University of Pennsylvania made a set of upper and lower teeth to my specifications, with which I immediately proceeded to eat foods which had previously been difficult for me to chew.* Once again I ate figs without seeds lodging under the denture!

"My theory has been proved correct. Where upper and lower dentures are required, the second molars should be removed from both plates. Dr. Victor H. Sears, Professor of Prosthetic Dentistry at the New York University College of Dentistry, wrote congratulating me on having solved a problem that baffled dentists for many years. As he remarked, '. . . strictly speaking, the problem was not a dental one but a problem in mechanics, which may account for the fact that dentists had attacked it from the wrong standpoint.' "

* "By eliminating the second molar entirely and leaving an open space in the back portion of the mouth, there is more room for the tongue in the open space where the molars had been, thus making it easy to propel food from the tongue to the cheek side and vice versa without forcing it against the flanges of the dentures.

"Stability comes from using twelve instead of fourteen teeth, leaving a hollowed open space in the back of the mouth, and eliminating pressure on the extreme ends of the plate. The occlusion becomes more centrally located (i.e., the occlusal balance is more closely approached where the chewing muscles are meant to receive that balance) and its (occlusal balance) support is increased by the extra length of the base plate reaching in the farthermost points of the gums' 'suction cup.'

"The open space behind the molar allows greater usefulness to the last tooth; and, aside from its natural function, it will increase its cutting angles like incisors because its back surface is completely uncovered."

WE GROW OLD . . . BECAUSE WE RUST OUT

Romano's views on how to live a long and happy life are based on his emotional attitude.

"Renewal of our cells does not stop when we grow old. It merely slows up. If we quicken the process of metabolism again, there seems to be no reason why we should not stay young as long as the renewed energy lasts. We grow old not because we wear out, but because we rust out. We grow tired of life; we become discouraged, discontented, unhappy, and ill, because we fail to make right use of the God-power within us."

TAKING LIFE SERIOUSLY

"I can't take everything seriously at my age (ninety-five). What is serious to someone else is a joke to me. It is the seriousness of children that causes them to cry. The parents say 'I wish I had his troubles.' But then the parent would have to be childish the rest of his life. As you grow up, the stereotyped forms of education, associated with etiquette, dressing, combing of the hair, and so forth, bring out artificial reactions and desires. Consequently you become serious."

TEN RULES FOR LONGEVITY

Romano once slowed down long enough to give his ten rules for longevity:

1. "To have your neighbors love you, show your consideration for others. You will then have self-respect.

2. "It is not what you are going to do, but what you have done.

3. "Treat people as if they were flowers, and you will have a happy life.

4. "By knocking others, you only practice self-degradation.

5. "Mind your own business and do not tell God what to do.

6. "Do not feel important, and do not take yourself seriously.

7. "Do not give advice without taking on responsibility.

8. "Avoid positive statements when discussing your philosophy of life. Do not argue with a fool, for if you do, two fools are arguing.

9. "Do not be anxious. Anything that irritates you is your master.

10. "Never eat at the same table with someone who nags you. Do not overeat at any one meal. Avoid foods hard to digest and the immoderate use of alcoholic beverages. If you smoke, do not inhale."

IV

DISCOVERING THE MAGNETIC
INFLUENCE OF SEX

*"Without romance it is not worth the trouble, and
with romance it is more trouble than it is worth."*

AS a young man Romano was dashing and mysterious.
Old photographs show him as a clean-shaven, handsome man-about-town, or a gentleman with a curled, black
moustache and dark, hypnotic eyes. Draped in oriental
toga or attired in evening dress, Romano captured the
hearts of operatic prima donnas and salesgirls, heiresses
and offspring of America's fledgling and Europe's de-
teriorating aristocracy.

His sure technique with the fair sex is shown in this
anecdote. "An office girl had been a big help to me in my
work. One day, while in an exuberant and grateful mood,
I suddenly kissed her on the cheek. She slapped my face.
I smiled and said, 'I am happy you did that, because I'd
rather have my face slapped by you than kissed by any
other girl.' From that day on she could never do enough
for me!"

Romano's zest for life found expression in passionate
impulses toward the fair sex. His vigor, virility, appetite,
and capacities in this realm remained strong throughout

his life. Much of his success with women might be attributed to his avoidance of dissipation and his genuine respect for their needs and feelings. He never solicited the companionship of a woman of dubious motives, but women sought him out. As a man of honor he never lied, broke promises, or subverted his supercharged mystic abilities to achieve any ungentlemanly ends. To the contrary, he remained aloof from many material and corrupting pleasures he could have had for the asking.

In his late forties Romano met his future wife at a social bridge game where he was reading palms for charity. Years later he told of how a stunning woman came in to have her palm read. "When I looked at her, I had the feeling that she was going to be my wife. I didn't know her name or where she lived. While reading her palm, I correctly described events of her past life and told her how unhappy she had been in her married life, and how she had attempted suicide on one or two occasions by threatening to jump out the window. I also told a lady friend of hers that a close relative had recently burned to death in Texas. It developed that it was the lady's sister and the tragedy had occurred two months previously."

Four or five weeks after this meeting Romano thought about "the beautiful lady," and soon after he had an unaccountable urge to take a walk along Riverside Drive. While sitting on a bench and daydreaming of the lady, he suddenly noticed some distance away an attractive woman walking a dog. "As she came closer I recognized her, but I made no effort to attract her attention. When she approached, she greeted me, then sat on the bench and talked to me. After a while I said, 'There is a way to be happy if you would look upon the sky as a roof to your house and the earth as a floor. This house has no need for doors, for your spirit will become the door to health, happiness, and contentment. Then and only then will you understand what Omar Khayyàm said: 'A jug of wine, a loaf of bread and thou.' Then, and only then, will you realize that happiness can never be bought with money. This very bench on which we are sitting is my home. Wherever I find peace of mind I am in my Garden of Eden. Only two people of the same mind can be happy. The day you can see the world as I see it will be the day we are happily married.' The beautiful lady had a beautiful soul. She told me her name and address and invited me to speak to her friends at a charity bridge game. Gradually we became better acquainted."

The beautiful lady, whose name was Molly, and Jacques Romano fell in love. Only a divorce from her "self-centered, well-to-do husband" stood in the way. Romano felt that, although her husband gave Molly everything that money could buy, he really did not care for her as a person. "He often left her for long periods without explanation. Even when at home, he virtually ignored her while playing bridge with his business acquaintances."

The divorce was complicated by the absence of Molly's husband, which made difficult the serving of the legal papers. However, Romano had a good hypnotic subject whom he put in a trance, and then, by traveling clairvoyance, he finally found the husband (see Chapter 10). The divorce was granted, and a little later Jacques Romano and Molly were married.

"The fact that Molly had parted from her husband and that I was well known both in Rochester and New York meant that if we were married in the United States the press might give it too much publicity. If we could be married in Canada that could be avoided. A Canadian law, however, required one to be a resident for a certain length of time before becoming eligible for a marriage license. We got around this because I was an honorary Commodore of a yacht club of the United States and Canada. When I told the authorities this, they were satisfied and let us get married. My friend, Mr. Clissold, helped with the arrangements and also gave the news to the Buffalo papers, June 13, 1914." The headline was:

"SCIENTIST WEDDED IN BRIDGEBURGH, ONTARIO.
JACQUES ROMANO TAKES AS WIFE
MRS. MOLLY MARSHALL."

The article said:

"Jacques Romano, well-known analytical chemist, of New York, and Mrs. Molly Marshall, formerly of Riverside Drive, New York City, now of Rochester, were quietly married at the Rectory of St. Paul's Episcopal Church, at Fort Erie, Ontario, at noon yesterday.

"Mr. Romano has been spending several weeks at Point Abino, Ontario, where the couple will pass part of the summer. The bride was attended by Mrs. Frederick Pohle, and the bridegroom by M. R. Clissold. The ceremony was performed by the Rev. Dr. McIntosh, Rector of St. Paul's.

"Mr. Romano has become conspicuous in scientific circles through his achievements in simplifying the production of sensitized paper in connection with photographic laboratories. Last year he was the guest of the Chamber of Commerce here, following his demonstration of mental phenomena before the National Council of Physicians and Surgeons at Pittsburgh. Mr. Romano is the inventor of a system now employed by the U.S. Federal Government for the verification of signatures and the detection of forgeries, and was a representative of the United States on the expedition under Professor Hewett to Yucatan. He is one of the few experts on therapeutic suggestion, though he does not follow the science as a profession. He has lectured before Columbia University in New York on this interesting department of metaphysics. After September, Mr. and Mrs. Romano will be at home in Pierpont Place, Rochester."

The marriage license gave Molly's age as thirty-seven and Jacques's as forty-one (actually their ages were forty-two and fifty). The reason for the inaccuracy of Jacques's given age is a story in itself. He always considered himself an American citizen "in body and soul," and never bothered to take out formal citizenship papers until one day in 1914 (before his marriage). Returning on a ship from South America, he noticed that a U.S. Consul was having trouble with immigration officials because he was without papers. Although Romano had never had trouble entering or leaving the United States previously and was successful this time because of the familiar Elk's pin he wore in his lapel ("You have to be a citizen to be a member of the Elks"), he decided to take out his papers at once.

The circuit judge in Rochester, New York, was amazed at "the little Spaniard" and advised him to take ten years off his age on the papers because "When you are older you will have a hard time getting a job." The judge asked Jacques about spirit readings, suggestive therapeutics, and his travels. He was baffled by Romano's youthful appearance and wondered if "it runs in the family." Romano said, "Molly and I finally decided to take nine years from my actual age. As a joker, I thought it would be fun also to change my real birthday, April 16th, to a national holiday, May 30th."

Jacques and Molly Romano had an uneventfully happy married life with no serious disharmony or friction. Mrs. Romano apparently adapted herself to her husband's remarkable personality and life. Finally, after forty-four years of marriage, she died.

Molly Romano, who was eight years her husband's junior, appeared to be many years older than her ninety-four-year-old husband. Many months before her health failed so rapidly, Romano correctly foretold the date of her death.* Besides Jacques's recurrent thoughts of suicide after his wife's death, another indication of the depth of his intense mourning for his wife was that he started to dream for the first time in his memory. These dreams had the recurrent theme of envisioning himself "on a boat going on a long voyage." He interpreted this as a wish to leave this world, his despondency, and his desire to find peace through death—the long voyage home.

* * *

Although he never personally practiced any sexual deviations, Romano was familiar with their existence and, in his own way, had quite a modern psychodynamic understanding of their causes. For instance, he felt that repeated early childhood experiences caused many of these illnesses: "The child cries, and the nurse rubs his genitals to quiet him. Then, children try these things with each other. Or, as another factor, I have known of society women who slept with their sons and of fathers who committed incest with their daughters. Much would also seem to depend on the culture. I remember how, in South America, at the turn of the century, mothers would occasionally offer me their daughters to sleep with when

* This information was supplied by a close personal friend of Romano.

I was a guest in their homes. . . . In sexual deviations . . . there is certainly much lying and whitewashing of the whole sad business. Many times the physicians are too stuffy or personally prejudiced with their own emotional values to listen to their patients and learn about these things.

"I was personally revolted by homosexuality. One of the few times in my life that I became very angry and could have knocked a man's teeth out was when such a man once put his hand on my knee. . . . It is a very hypocritical condition. They (homosexuals) are very sick people. Their underlying problems are emotional and center on hatred. There is no warmth or genuine affection. Their love is a sham for the tremendous hostility, corruption, and often violence that they inwardly harbor. Ugh! They need the help of a psychiatrist!"

Romano, in his inimitable manner, also made some remarks on sexual function in general. For example, "Mr. Romano, my son is engaged to a woman my wife and I do not approve of. What can we do for the boy? Can you tell us how we can reason with him?"

"You cannot reason with a man when he is having an erection," was Romano's sage reply.

"For many people sex is purely physical and nothing emotional. For example, every man and woman has an odor, and that is a basic (biological) and often overlooked reason for the attraction between the two sexes. Sex is a creative energy. That is why inventors and thinkers are often frigid men and why there have been so few inventors in Turkey. There, sex is used for dissipation and not procreation. Sex is exercised on (their) many wives and concubines. In our society it is often an unhappy marriage when the husband has creative energy and does not expend it on his wife. Sex, as a creative energy, should never be abused. It gives maximum gratification to both the man and the woman when it functions in harmonious concert with the emotions.

"However, when sex dies, never let affection die. Sex is one thing and affection another. Affection has a magnetic influence that can recharge the vitality and strength of a person, whereas sex, misused, can weaken it. As you grow older, you cannot rejuvenate yourself, but you can always stimulate affection which will make living worthwhile. You'll be beloved by people and feel warmly toward them. Affection can be continued and strengthened throughout all of life."

*   *   *

The following vignettes characterize Romano's views on relationships between the sexes.

ELLA WHEELER WILCOX, AMERICAN POETESS

"Ella Wheeler Wilcox believed in reincarnation and spiritualism. She felt that she and her husband would work for humanity in the hereafter. Ella was good-hearted and hoped that her writing would enable people to better understand themselves and each other. She used to call me an 'old soul.' Because I did not disagree with her, she was fond of me. She was a frail little woman with many wrinkles on her face. Once, when I saw her sitting in the lobby of the Hotel Astor, I tiptoed up to her and kissed her on the forehead. I said, 'Ella, when I look at your face I'm inspired. Many people try to get rid of their wrinkles, but the lines carved on your face represent the wisdom and beauty of thousands of years.'"

ANNE MORGAN, SISTER OF J. P. MORGAN

"I used to visit Anne Morgan nearly every week. She invited me to her cocktail parties. She liked me and enjoyed my company. Anne could come right to the point. I once received a letter from her in which she said, 'I know you walk up 28 flights of stairs to your office at John Hays Hammond's for exercise so why can't you walk up only eight floors to my office once in a while?'

"On a different occasion she said to me, 'Look here, Jacques! You always tell everybody things about their nature and past. Why don't you tell me something?' I said, 'I would be happy to tell you. Anne Morgan, you are the most selfish woman I have ever met in my life!' She exploded, 'This is the last time you and I will ever have a drink together! Get the hell out of here!' I purred, 'Wait! Let me explain. Selfishness can be constructive or destructive. You are the most selfish woman I ever met in helping people to get the things they need the most. You will not let anyone else know about this glorious quality. It is most beautiful. Your selfishness exists for the happiness and benefit of other people.' Anne's unusually husky, rather masculine voice softened, 'Jacques, you can stay here and drink whenever and as long as you want.'"

MEN WHO RUN AROUND

"People often ask me why it is not uncommon for a man between fifty and sixty years of age to play around with young girls. I answer that the laws of men are made to accommodate (biological) institutions, but such rules frequently become far distant from the nature of man. For instance, it is the (biological) nature of man to be a polygamist and for a woman to be a monogamist. A man possesses much more creative energy for reproduction than a woman. A healthy man can (theoretically) mate with three hundred women and sire three hundred children in a year, whereas a woman can have three hundred men but give birth to only one child, or, rarely, have a multiple birth. So the man has the ability to propagate many offspring, but the laws of man harass and subdue his natural desires.

"It should also be noted that the function of creative energy is so sensitive that the slightest negligence can cause a disturbance. For instance, it is the deep and true affairs of the heart, the passions of love and hate, even though not openly expressed, spoken of, or understood that account for the changes in sexual function. The conditions of impotence and frigidity stem from these confused and often hidden emotions.

"On the other hand when there is an affinity between a young man and woman, or 'love at first sight,' there is a companionship of such opposite polarity, feeling, and truthfulness that the two people wish to give life to a body (the unborn baby) which does not yet exist. Or, conversely, maybe there might be a life (force) without that finds it congenial to have a body created by this couple in love. Here intercourse is not cultivated but is something of nature. The truest love is always 'love at first sight.' There is an old saying, 'Only illegitimate children are smart.' In this instance, then, there is no motive, just love. Thus, when lovers hold hands they speak a language without words, which beautifully expresses their shared affection and symbolizes their wish that they will never be parted.

"To continue with the question why a man between fifty and sixty sometimes turns to young girls, it should be noted that a healthy man has intercourse from one to three times a week. And every time he has intercourse with a woman he can produce life, but this is not so with a woman. It is my observation that as long as a woman is able to become pregnant the man and the woman have intercourse not only with orgasm but also with the propensity for stimulating the 'life touch.' They are both sensitive to the 'life touch' without knowing what it is. When a woman goes into the menopause, she can still have orgasm during intercourse, but she no longer has the 'life touch.' Therefore, the man who is still able to produce a new life runs to young girls because the spark of life is lacking in the older woman. When a man and woman have lived their lives together with an enduring exchange of affection, the man does not become wayward. Therefore, when sex dies, never let affection die."

THE FAIR SEX, A HUMAN CALENDAR

"A woman is never satisfied. She works, saves her money, and then buys a nice dress. Two weeks later, after wearing the dress, she cries because the style has changed. According to the law of Nature, though, a woman must be patient. For instance, when she begins to have menstrual periods, she knows what will happen every month. If there is a delay she becomes excited.

"Nature has also made her impatient. At a certain age

she knows she should marry, for if she is not married by that time, she will be an old maid. If she has become a widow or a divorcee, she should have a better chance, because she knows about the physical aspects of marriage. When a woman marries, she counts the months until she has a baby. When she is pregnant she seems restless. This is due to her maternal protective instinct and can be illustrated from nature. When a pregnant cheetah dashes hither and yon in the dark, it is not because of restlessness, as the natives maintain, but for the protection of the unborn puppy. A domesticated cat will usually choose a place where one would never expect her to have her kittens. In the wilderness deer are born in desolate, isolated areas surrounded by swamp or bramble. Possibly a verbal carryover of this protective maternal instinct is the woman's often heard comment, 'I don't trust that man!' Finally, after the birth, the mother counts the time until the baby turns over, sits up, has its first tooth, and so on. When the child has grown, the woman repeats the cycle again with the grandchild. The fair sex is a human calendar, from the beginning to the end."

THE THREE LOVES OF WOMAN

"Each woman can love three men in her life. Her first love is for a man of strength. This is her real love. The second love is economic. It is for a man of security. This is an artificial love. And the third love is for a man of genius. She wants something different and is saturated with sex from the first or second love. Wanting a man whom she can respect for his accomplishments, she then falls in love with a genius of some kind."

COSMETICS

"Of all the animals, only among humans does the female wear gayer plumage than the male. Since females, like the lower animals, are charged with the responsibility of looking after the offspring, the males have to lure them —hence the mane of the lion and the tail of the peacock and the glorious plumage of the other birds. But in civilization, woman beguiles man because of the law that compels him to support her and the children. Thus, the ever present market for cosmetics."

GARBO—REJUVENATOR OF WOMEN

"Gustafson, known under the name of Garbo, originated a method of giving to elderly women with wrinkled faces, a smooth, white, youthful skin. Both here and in England many of his rejuvenations were amazingly successful. He was a most unusual man. He was honest, and his word was as good as gold. He was a first-generation Swede from Montana, whose father was a Lutheran pastor. His father was so devout that he insisted his children learn their prayers in Hebrew.

"As a boy, Gustafson was delicate and sickly. He told me that his body often became so overheated that he would have to step outside naked in the snow in order to cool off. As a boy, he was teased and bullied by the neighborhood ruffians, because he could not fight. He made up his mind to learn how to fight, and he developed such strength that no one dared cross him. He was cool in his manner and spoke in a calm, mellow way—like putting a needle through your body. He never raised his voice. One day, he met a man who was rather vulgar. Gustafson, who could not stand such people, said, 'You need not say any more. I know your background. Your mother was conceived in a pigsty.'

"Early in his career Gustafson was prospecting out West. He became a shrewd observer. That is what we had in common and why we got along so well. He told me how he once was camping in a cold, mountainous area known for rattlesnakes. When he went to sleep he felt something crawling under his feet. By Jove! He noticed that rattlesnakes had come into the tent and under his quilt. He said that he did not bother them but just moved more slowly. He realized that the rattlers had come in to warm themselves against his body.

"Once we were riding the subway together. Gustafson got up and courteously offered his seat to a lady, but a big burly man sat down first. Gustafson said, 'I did not give you this seat, I gave it to the lady.'

"The brute shot back, 'Well, I'm sitting here now, I'm tired and I want to sit.'

"Gustafson: 'I want you to understand that I gave this seat to the lady, and I do not wish to have any confusion about this. Will you please get up and give this seat to the lady?'

" 'No, sir, I don't want to.'

" 'I'll ask you once more.' Then Gustafson's face flushed, and he got fire in his eyes. Reaching over, he picked the burly brute up and threw him on the floor! Gustafson had quite a grip. He developed it out West. He hated dishonesty, discourtesy, and violence. Gustafson was always a gentleman and one to be reckoned with."

V

OVERCOMING GRIEF AND FEAR

"Hate is a slow process of committing suicide. It is foolish to hate someone and die for him."

AFTER his grandfather's death, Jacques, who was then eight years old, began to brood. Many years later he described his feelings: "I began to philosophize. All the children were devoted to each other. I knew how families grew up, loved, and then were parted. My brothers and sisters, and then some day my own children, would see me die. Why should one live and have children? I thought."

In his despondency Jacques attempted suicide by hanging. However, some servants heard him gagging and ran to the room just in time to cut him down. His stolid parents had little to say about this near tragedy. But from then on the servants were carefully watching him. They treated him like a precocious child. At this early age Jacques made up his mind never to get married and have children. "I saw life as a tragedy and a world of sorrow. On my birthday I felt that it was not a celebration but that I had one year less to live."

Many years later while looking at these particular notes,

Romano said, "I wrote this sixty-six years ago. I had been in the United States only a short time and I was down and out and living on the Bowery. This was the second time in my life that I felt like committing suicide.

"Then a simple event occurred that I could not understand but which changed my mind and lifted my spirits. I saw an old Italian lady with a sorrowful, worried face. I helped her put a bundle on her back and then, suddenly, I said to myself, 'Why should I, a young man, think of suicide? *Cabeza dura* (blockhead)!'

"This seemingly trivial experience brought about a great change in me for the better. Yet, I could not help but wonder about the melancholy thoughts I had recently put down on paper. Now as I read these notes of sixty-six years ago, I said to myself: 'Such beautiful foolishness! *Cabeza dura.*'

"The death of my grandfather became an obsession. I knew something of life, but death loomed as a great venture. Life seemed meaningless to me. I did not want to live. I did not want to live the experiences of my father and the last years of my grandfather. Death calmed me. I was so peaceful. The sadness of it all gratified me.

"In death I looked forward to a new companionship, a departure from my present surroundings, a sort of transformation. In the vastness of death there are new experiences, new realizations. Wanting to end life, I decided to hang myself. I decided to experiment with hanging in the attic, the place of my retreat. The attic had many crossbeams the full length of the room. It seemed an ideal place to hang myself. The attic was my place of retreat to silence, the something that urged me to find a solution to the many questions that crowded my mind.

"There I would roam around the old discarded things

which had outlived their usefulness. Somehow I felt—
there was life. The old coffers filled with broken statuary
inspired me with a past life. They wanted me to realize
something. Old furniture had the same story for me. So
did the old musical instruments, especially an antique
broken violin. To this day the thought of it makes me sad.
The violin made me melancholy. When I touched it, I
felt tense and old. Yet I always wanted to hold it and pat
it. I held it in an embrace, tighter and tighter. My eyes
would fill with tears, and still I was not weeping. In my
grief I would try to find a new resting place for the violin.
Not a hiding place, just a resting place.

"In that attic I practiced hanging myself. I would put
a rope around my neck, close my eyes, think of my parents, of kissing my little sisters and brothers goodbye, and
then bend my knees until I experienced a choking sensation. My face would feel swollen. I would feel dizzy.

"Then, somehow I did not want to die in the attic. The
place was depressing and lonely. I wanted to die in happy
surroundings, so I decided to die in the children's play-
room. I wanted to be found dead by my laughing sisters
and brothers. Their cry of horror would mean they had
much sympathy for me. I wanted their impression of
death. I felt they would give me their utmost, an intensity
of something. I wanted them to be very, very close to me.
I wanted to be in the midst of their sorrow a long time
before I was buried. I did not want a quick parting. It
frightened me when I pictured their departure from the
cemetery, leaving me alone in the grave. Their sadness
meant a greater love for me, a newer kind of love, a love
only death could bring, and a love that comes with a
newly born life.

"I enjoyed every imaginary sensation that my death

would bring. I knew that my cousins would also feel sorry and sad. That pleased me very much. Their sorrow I interpreted as a sort of remorse. I enjoyed this remorse. I wanted them to be frightened. I wanted them to vividly see me being eaten up by the worms. I wanted them to be terribly sorry.

"As for my parents, since they were responsible for my birth, I thought my death could be transformed by them into a greater love for the other children. That was all I could think. To me, this was added justification for my committing suicide."

Jacques made little further comment about his second episode of depression when he was in the United States sixty-six years earlier. However, by reflecting on the child-hood suicide attempt and going so far as to write about it, Jacques overcame his depression and remained well until his ninety-fourth year when, after forty-four years of mar-riage, his wife died.

Most of his friends had long since died. He had no im-mediate family and could only foresee a monotonous rou-tine of working hard in his laboratory all day, then han-dling his business and personal correspondence in the loneliness of a small apartment at night.

In these somber surroundings, in the twilight of a ven-erable age, the great struggle erupted again between the will for life and the desire for escape and peace through death. As in the earlier crises, the will to live triumphed. It was fortified by a sardonic humor combined with shrewd insights. The shock of losing his life mate, com-panion, and friend was overcome by the ability to go over all his past feelings toward his wife. He shared some of these positive and negative sentiments in their varying complexity with his friends.

In his mourning, he reviewed a long married life: the happy times, dinners with friends, trips abroad, everyday petty disagreements, and in later years the agonies of being separated by biological age difference when still so close spiritually.

"People who commit suicide are like those who suffer from headaches. One person takes a sleeping powder for relief, and the other a headache powder. Neither one finds out the cause of his disturbance. The one who commits suicide by jumping out the window is afraid of changing his mind, or really understanding himself, his true feelings and motivation.

"This is a time (Molly's death) that I have to work out my own salvation. I must overcome this grief myself, and become stronger for the days ahead. I am a realist, and nobody can advise me on what to do. If I don't get over this I'll commit suicide. I'm at home, by myself, lonely, and miles from where my wife's ashes are. Now I can only communicate with sand.

"When the undertaker asked me what particular clergyman I wished to take the funeral service, I said, 'My wife was a good woman. God knows that. My wife doesn't need someone else to tell God what a good woman she was.' Since Molly's death I've lost all patience. Death is a release to an aged man; and to his friends of the younger generation it is also a release."

Gradually, with the passage of time, and with the influence of many fond memories, good friends, and the demands of his occupation and active life, Romano worked through the depths of his great loss. Although he sorely missed his wife, the will to live reasserted itself. He now felt freer than he had in years to accept invitations to travel and lecture on his unusually good health and amazing telepathic powers. Now he could stay overnight with friends who had been put off for years because of Molly Romano's infirmities. Thus, despite the taboo usually associated with a nonagenarian existence, Romano resumed his old furious pace in his daily work, while still finding time to fly to the Pacific Coast and speak at a college commencement, take a Caribbean cruise with physicians, attend monthly dinners at his Medical Strollers Club, and give countless benefit performances for both young and old.

On such occasions, Romano, the natural aristocrat, would wear his familiar single-breasted black suit, navy blue clip-on bow tie, and Prince Albert-style vest. When the guests arrived, they met a small, straight-backed, wiry gentleman with black-rimmed glasses. He would spring to his feet and in a clear confident voice, with engaging elegance and courtesy, he would participate in the usual social amenities. Then, with a sudden twinkle in his eyes, he would shake hands with the guests and disarm them by his rapidfire volley of quips and inspired flashes of mind reading.

By his unorthodox but highly effective comments and behavior, Romano showed his audiences how he learned to reduce tension by refraining from hate. He fascinated them with much helpful advice based on experiences from his long life. Many of those who listened to him smiled and chuckled after seeing how Romano could put them in a different perspective. Through his sprightly delivery and delightful sense of humor they learned how to help dissolve their own cares and worries. It was always exciting to hear how, through patience and understanding, Romano could transform fear into knowledge and wisdom.

"When I am introduced to physicians, they enjoy being

told that I know they want to meet me to find out why I
don't die and how they can live longer. If I am introduced
to an undertaker, I ask him how he can pray to God for
more business. I tell the guests that I remain young in my
nineties by having a new love affair every day. That there
are some people I meet whom I love to be with, and other
people I meet whom I love to be without. It is my mission
to live as long as possible, because with each successive
year I become more valuable to people who can see me as
an example of what can be done. It gives them more hope
than anything I know."

Another favorite bit of repartee about the question of
longevity was this: "I'm always dying; I'm not living. I
want to die happily and if I'm through with somebody,
I'm through. I have never spent time with a fool. In this
way I always benefit. I never lose, and I cannot fear death
because I have been rehearsing dying without knowing
that I am alive. I'm prepared to stop waking up. I live
and become, with each successive year, more immune to
the destructive bombardment of the senses which can be
subconsciously crippling.

"I am thinking of living to three hundred years! Unfortunately for most people, a statement of deep suggestive
effect was made by a wise man thousands of years ago. By
his proclaiming the biblical three score and ten as the
norm, he destroyed the hope of a long life for human
beings and made them die a premature death. Therefore,
today, when a man is forty-five he is already buying a plot
in the cemetery, waiting for his future home; and, when
he is between sixty-five and seventy, people say he looks
like he'll soon die; and when he is more than seventy, he
goes around with a smile on his face, joking, 'I'm living
on borrowed time!' which means, 'I'll die any day now.'

"If this wise man of long ago had understood suggestive therapeutics, he would have said that the span of life for a human being, compared to animals, extends to a hundred and twenty years. So by my reckoning, at seventy years of age I would then have fifty more years to go. That is why I feel and act like a youngster who has three hundred years to live! If I die in the meantime I would never know it, and all the while I would be having a whale of a good time. Besides, why should I care about the gossip, for I have read of my death in the newspapers several times?

"It seems to me that the human animal has several ways to shorten his life. They are, chiefly, fear, worry, hurry, and hate.

"My parents implanted in their children the destructive twins of fear and hate, but they were no different from other parents who acquire their understanding through traditional education, which in turn really derives from paganism. It is fear that leads to the anticipation and elaboration of a perverted and fanatical education. The reaction of fear originally came to us by way of Nature's own destructive elements: cyclones, earthquakes, floods, typhoons, fires, and epidemics. I believe that fear accounted for the sadistic concepts of Hell, evil spirits, devils, ghosts, and myriad superstitions; and the fear of manmade evils, wars, criminals, murderers, and corruption is related to these furies of nature. Any one or a combination of these factors is enough to shorten a man's life.

"With the repeated sorrows that come with destruction and misfortune, our fears of the unexpected and of the expected gradually numb our senses of self-preservation, and we look forward to the 'three score and ten' for relief as a means to the end of a finite existence. But this 'three score and ten' should be merely a symbol of having reached an age of understanding and wisdom where the past turmoils die and life begins again, closer to the Infinite Law, instead of the disturbed finite existence which ends with death. By letting the Infinite influence our destiny we learn many things unknown in our finite existence.

"In our lives some minutes never seem to end. The happy years appear to pass quickly, and the uncertain minutes move slowly in space and time. With experience we adjust ourselves to the visible destructive elements of Nature and Man. However, although we subconsciously try to cast aside the inferno which Dante described and Doré illustrated, we find it hard to overcome the fear that stems from a mind poisoned with tales of Hell and its like. As a cruel result of these fantasies of a wild imagination, this usual early sadistic education can become destructive to our lives. Therefore, for myself, I've tried to overcome this deadly influence by fighting fire with fire.

"Fortified by calmness, I allowed my mind to wander with full power of imagination to every form of self-destruction. I lived every torture ascribed to the flames of Hell. I lived each phase with gusto and reality. Mentally I sank into the deep sea, to the bottom of the black ocean. I lived every form of danger among the creatures of the depths: I allowed myself to be devoured by them and then survived to live those experiences over again. On earth I placed myself within the forest fires, within the cyclones, in the cracks of volcanos, and in the floods where I was constantly pummeled by wreckage. In snake pits I have been struck by poisonous fangs—yes, I lived it all, over and over again. I've lived all of the forms of imaginary fears inherited from our ancestors who worshipped bloodthirsty gods. But there was less fear to overcome in the world of nature than in that of the mind."

In addition to overcoming the ravages of nature and the terrors of a manmade Hell, Romano obtained victory over melancholy and achieved longevity by other means. Through attaining self-mastery and developing a keen awareness of his emotional reactions with other people, he learned how to keep tension at a minimum and thus function more efficiently.

What he had to say is provocative of fresh insights for anyone who wants to live happily. "My temperament does not let me hate. Hate is a slow process of committing suicide. It is foolish to hate someone and die for him. Usually if there is no hate, there is no fear. Why should I aggravate myself and hasten the aging process? Aging comes by dissipation, catering, and overdoing things, taking oneself too seriously. I have no anxiety. I do not know how to be angry or disappointed; I can find an excuse for everybody.

"If you treat people like flowers, you'll have a happy life. Anything that I dislike dominates me, but when I understand it, I dominate the situation. I like to meet obnoxious and vulgar people, for they show me how different I am and teach me self-control. My greatest self-importance is to lose self-importance and be on the level of everyone I meet.

"Anxiety robs you of patience and composure. Anxiety and ambition shorten your life. Look in the mirror and you see your worst enemy. I am rich, because everything in the world is mine. The flowers in the garden and the grain in the fields are mine, but others look after them.

"The laws of adaptation and harmony teach me to face danger, handle fear, and dissolve hate. My religious outlook becomes a response to my inner identity which never ends. I believe that Great Law established by the Infinite Intelligence. The power to which I bow is called by many names: Al, Allah, Dios, God, Gott.

"Religions to me are just various forms of ceremonies, many of which are adapted from paganism. I shall follow the Master and pray in my inner self with words unspoken: We serve God by serving mankind."

VI

BELIEFS, INSIGHTS, AND
INTERPRETATIONS

*"You cannot change your religion; you only change the
ceremony."*

R OMANO practiced what he preached. Clergymen of all
faiths sought his opinions. People of varying points of
view were often surprised to discover a greatly expanded
self-awareness after hearing Romano's interpretations of
biblical passages and his own life experiences.

They found his views on life, death, and religion of
practical "here and now" significance. Subjects that they
had been taught as children at home, church, and elsewhere took on new dimensions. For many people his comments proved most beneficial for everyday living. Though
his opinions were often highly original, they were presented in a straightforward manner.

For example, years after Romano's death it was a common experience to receive inquiries about how the in-
quirer could obtain material on Romano's philosophy.
Those who had heard him speak, or read some of his quotations in various pamphlets and posters, treasured his
wholesomeness and found an exciting transfusion of life
in his expressed beliefs.

Although Romano often mixed a dash of humor or bite

in his interpretations of religious stories and events, no one objected. On the contrary, he could hold an audience spellbound. His audiences were often groups connected with churches and synagogues. They were not overconcerned with the precise rightness or wrongness, historical accuracy, and the like, of what he said, for they found Romano had a worthwhile message—timely yet timeless.

In his own words, the following typify what Romano believed and what he really was.

WHAT RELIGION?

"People ask 'What religion are you?' I say, 'Be patient, watch my behavior and not what I claim to be. Find out if I'm honest, if I'm happy, if I drink—then religion does not mean much. How can you blame anyone for their religion when they were raised in it? You cannot change your religion; you only change the ceremony. All religions are alike to the one who loves God instead of fearing Him.'

"I do not entertain wishful thinking. I do not take stimulants. My prayers are not for a jug of wine and a loaf of bread. My prayer is for the wisdom to follow the Law of Righteousness without a prescribed policy and to be master of the physical and mental."

CREDO

"Romano, which is the best religion?"

"The religion that produces the least number of criminals."

"What church do you go to, Romano?"

"Why should I go to church? Do you mean to tell me that God is hiding in a church? When I was a child they told me that God was everywhere."

"A remorseful prayer needs no vocabulary."

"To have your neighbors love you shows your consideration for others."

"God, give me sense, and I will not bother you."

"What makes you so healthy at ninety-five, Romano?"

"Very simple, I mind my own business and do not tell God what to do."

"I'd rather have you hate me for telling the truth than love me for lying."

"Patience is the door to self-mastery. It is the road to the Infinite within us."

GOD AND THE DEVIL

"According to some theology, God tells the Devil how to torture people in Hell. Some people believe that God condemns a sinner to purgatory and torture. Thus, theology makes God an accessory to all the tortures, crimes, and sadisms of Hell, and the willfulness of the Devil. How can anyone expect me to reform as a sinner if the Devil, who has been in the company of God for infinite time, is not reformed yet?"

GOD OR MAN

"All that I heard as a child contradicted itself. I had a French governess who said, 'Be careful, Jacques, God knows everything you think and do.' I believed it. One day I told her I wanted some special thing. She said, 'Pray to God, and He will give it to you.' I said, 'If He knows my every thought, why should I have to pray?' I started to think. I could not believe that God, who was so kind, would associate with the Devil in Hell. How could He make the Devil do all the dirty work?

"I found out that Hell and all its threats are very destructive to a person's conscience and righteousness. Man is forced to be good not by a natural self-respect and consideration for others, but because he is being bribed. 'Be good and you'll be rewarded, you will go to Heaven and have a wonderful time.' God knows the righteousness and wrongfulness of every human being. Why does God need a lawyer (preachers, etc.) to tell Him these things? This I could not see."

THE LIFE HEREAFTER

"When I was ninety-five, a priest asked me if I believed in the resurrection. I said, 'Yes and no.' When we are born on this earth we have a finite existence. At death we have a resurrection to an infinite existence. I then continued, 'Now, Father, if you mean resurrection to a state resembling our bodily existence, I am doubtful. Let us find out about everyone who has lived on this earth and died. First, no one who has died has come back. I see no reason to come back and meet those I love since they are also dead. Now, Father, you must have brothers and sisters, close relatives, and friends—how often do you visit them? Do you mean to tell me it is worthwhile coming back to meet the same people you now keep away from?' "

SELF-MASTERY

"Self-mastery needs no weapons or muscles; anyone who can find companionship within himself, alone, can develop self-mastery. This is illustrated in the animal kingdom. The elephant is big and powerful, but the lion will attack him; so the elephant goes in herds, thus showing his weakness and need for companionship. The same might be said for sheep, gazelles, and other herbivorous animals. A lion is considered the king of beasts because he is master of himself and can travel alone.

"An ostrich, who can kick a human being down, needs companionship, so ostriches go in flocks. The eagle is master of himself; he never goes in flocks but, like the lion, travels alone. Anyone who can travel alone and does not need companionship to stimulate his self-confidence has reached the highest form of self-discipline and mastery. Jesus was unknown during eighteen of his formative years and I believe that it was then that he developed the same self-mastery. Many great men develop it themselves by going into isolation, but the mastery of physical and mental strength should not be confused with the eccentricities of a hermit who merely vegetates."

JESUS THE JEW

"One December, I was strolling down Pennsylvania Avenue in Washington, D.C. On the corner was a Salvation Army group beating their drums and tambourines, and singing. Among the many people standing around was a tipsy observer who, in a thick brogue, ridiculed the singer. 'Look at these people in their little hats making so much noise. They don't even know what they're talking about.' I answered him with a biblical quotation of Jesus to the effect that he should be tolerant and shut up for a while, but he could not hold his tongue and started again: 'That such rabble should be out on the street begging!' Again I quoted another saying of Jesus, but this only made him angrier. He said, 'Where do you come in quoting from Jesus? You look like a Jew!' I turned and complimented him with a smile, 'Thank you for your generosity. Jesus looked more like a Jew than one of your kind!' "

GOD-AL-ALLAH

"Many of the Protestant sects obtain strength in their belief about the name of God—Jehovah (Yahweh). Yet, how can you have a name for God when He is an identity which has always existed? The reason that we want to give it a name is because we wish to have a better contact with the intelligent, creative energy. In my interpretation, God is beyond human comprehension. It is an infinite intelligence. For mortals to even try to define it further is futile.

"The name for God must have started long before the days of Abraham. The ancient peoples felt that God represented life, and that He gave them life to exist in Him. They might have wondered, 'Where is the real life located in the human body?' They might have noted that they were not particularly sensitive to blows on the head, legs, arms, or back, but if struck in the pit of the stomach they would collapse and have difficulty breathing.

"In the Orient I observed that both Jews and Arabs frequently carry packages on top of their heads and thus they further protect this relatively insensitive part of the body and also free their hands for other purposes, such as gesticulating and defense. The package acts like a helmet and protects them from immediate collapse if they are struck on the head.

"Orientals might have noticed that when they cut the head off some animal like a chicken, it still runs and jumps about. The ancients came to believe, therefore, that the sensitive part of life was centered in the solar plexus, the central part of the body, and it was associated with breathing.

"When the early Hebrews prayed to God, who represented the supreme power or life without, they wanted to use the life within themselves as a contact. They wanted to make a sound echoing their basic breathing experience of life communicating with a life. They used the word 'Al' which sounded as if they were breathing very heavily and feeling the effect in the pit of their stomachs. Thus, 'Al' became the symbolic word for God and the real God that the Hebrews used to pray to. When Jesus was crucified, He cried, 'Eli, Eli' (My God, My God).

"When the Arabs came along and realized that 'Al' stood for God, they doubled it, as if breathing in and out, and called it 'Allah.' In Hebrew prayer today, the ancient 'Al' is still recognizable. They say, 'Jehovah Elohim' (Creator, Our Lord).

"Our English word 'God' comes from the Goths, who made stone idols. When the tribes they conquered came in contact with these idols, they called them 'Goths,' or gods of the Goths. In the Spanish language the sun worshippers called their gods 'Dios' or daylight—the sungod.

"In making idols the Egyptians found that the higher

and more impressive the statue, the greater the effect of the prayer. When the worshipper holds his head up and his mouth open, he enters a trancelike state in which his mind becomes a blank. He is relieved from all distractions, sorrows, and worries."

TALKING WITH THE HANDS

"Why did the Jews, Arabs, Greeks, and Armenians use their hands when talking?"

"Because their vocabulary was so limited and lacking in descriptive words that they had to supplement their few words by using their hands for giving directions, counting, indicating size, and for emotional states associated with fighting, disapproval, approval, and so forth."

THE SACRIFICIAL LAMB

"In all the different parts of the world where I traveled, I studied the animal life. From the Bible I learned that there were sheepherders who inhabited tropical lands. This puzzled me and I wondered why sheep in warm, tropical countries had need for so much wool. I also questioned why the people ate sheep and a few goats rather than other animals. My observations ran contrary to these climatic conditions.

"This apparent paradox was resolved when I concluded that the sheep, per unit of weight, has less blood than other animals. He therefore needs the wool for warmth. I also noticed that sheep do not usually develop chronic diseases, but more often die from conditions of sudden onset. For this reason, then, the ancients believed that the sheep was one of the healthiest of animals and safe for eating. If the sheep died within a short time, it must have been diseased and the meat became unfit for eating. This is one of the reasons why the lamb, of all animals, was most frequently offered in sacrificial feasts and became one of the food staples in the Orient."

HELL

"There is no Hell, Purgatory, or torture in the Old Testament. The terrifying concept of a 'fire and brimstone' Hell is theological sadism concocted from the New Testament. However, in order to prove there is a Hell, the theologians picked out Gehenna in the Valley of Hinam, outside the city of Jerusalem. Gehenna, translated 'Hell' in the New Testament, was a burning place for trash and an ancient site for child sacrifice. This concept of Hell was well known to the Chinese and Babylonians. The Jews may have developed their ideas of Hell when they were captured by the Babylonians and reduced to slavery. The word Hell itself simply means 'grave.' As an illustration, the old saying, 'I'd rather go to Hell than do anything wrong,' originally meant, 'I'd rather die than do anything bad.' "

HEBREW JUSTICE

"If a man who committed murder or any crime with a death penalty escaped to a 'safety zone' in Palestine and was allowed to remain there, the authorities would not

molest him. The criminal would have to work for his re-
demption among his criminal peers.

"Here is another Talmudic example of justice: If a man
stole a sheep, he paid with one sheep; if he stole an ox,
he paid with seven. The ancients felt that, if a man stole
a sheep at night, he could not drive it but would have to
carry it on his shoulders. Taking this into consideration,
the early Hebrew judges ruled that the thief had already
suffered enough. However, if he stole an ox, it was an
easy thing to drive it away; and that is why he had to pay
with seven oxen."

HEBREW LANGUAGE

"In studying different languages I found that the Hebrew characters had no connection with any other ancient
script. I concluded that they symbolically portrayed the
evolution of the earth. The *aleph,* א, represents the
double swastika. It includes the male and female together
as the clockwise and counterclockwise flags.

"The rest of human progress is also illustrated by the
letters of the Hebrew alphabet. *Beth* (Greek Beta), ב, is
a house. The character represents a cave dug in the mountain. *Gimel* (Greek Gamma), ג, shows a hammer and
claw to pry open, an early tool. *Daleth* (Greek Delta), ד,
is the first carpenter's angle used in building.

"*He* (Greek Epsilon), ה, illustrates the first house and
its particular type of entrance. In the earliest dwellings
entry was made from the top by means of a rope. This
was to protect the occupants from invaders. Some of the
Coptic monasteries I visited in Africa still had these kinds
of homes.

"*Vau* and *Zayin*, ו ז, showed two kinds of wooden nails used in these early buildings. *Cheth*, ח, portrays how the house has evolved because now there is an entrance, or as the character shows, a doorway. The rest of the letters may well have a similar origin. Special attention should be given to the letter *Shin* ש, which illustrates the triad and is the first letter of the Hebrew word *Shadei*, meaning God Almighty. *Shin* has the same mystical meaning as the pyramids."

SWASTIKA

"The swastika is a widespread sign found in ancient Oriental civilizations and known by its Sanskrit name. The swastika is also a primitive cross. In tracing its origin and interpreting its symbolic meaning, I noted its resemblance to the first letter of the Hebrew alphabet, *aleph*, א. In the early development of the language, a curve symbolized instability; and a straight line, stability. In oriental designs, a dot in the center with four curved parallel lines radiating from it can often be seen. This represents the earth in the making, a cauldron of liquid fire.

"According to the ancients, the earth cooled off in the center; they represented this as a cross with curves on the ends. This indicated that the outside of the world was still in its fiery liquid form. Then, when the earth became a solid instead of a curve, they made straight lines, or, as you see, a swastika. When the earth produced life, however, something was needed to symbolize the two sexes. This was done by having the flags turn counterclockwise for the female and clockwise for the male."

YOGI AND GOY

"Yogi is a Hebrew word derived from the magic number 13, and is symbolic of the highest form of intelligence. Until his son is thirteen, the father is responsible for his son's sins; the boy is then confirmed and, thereafter, directly responsible to God for his own sins. The Hebrews believed a boy entered manhood at the age of thirteen and would attain the highest form of intellectual status and belief in God. Thirteen is also a mystic number. Jacob and his twelve children equaled thirteen, as did Jesus and Buddha, each with their twelve disciples.

"Yogi comes from the tenth letter, *yodh,* and *gimel,* the third letter of the Hebrew alphabet. In Greek it is the numeral for 10, iota, and the third letter, gamma, respectively. Ten and three; *yodh* and *gimel,* make thirteen. When these two are combined, they are pronounced in English as in Hebrew: *yog, yoga,* and *yogi.* The reverse spelling of 'yog' is 'goy,' or 3 and 10, which also equals the mystic number 13. *Gimel* and *yodh,* or 'goy,' means a Gentile, an intelligent man, but among Jews signifying one who is not a *yog* or a confirmed Jew."

SHEENEY

"Sheeney is derived from another name for God that the Jews never use but which is written in their scrolls in halfsize. It comes from *Shadei,* which means 'God Almighty.' *Shin,* שׁ, is a Hebrew holy letter and represents the triangle because of the three dots on top.

"In Spain, the Jews could not reveal their religion; many even had crucifixes on their door. But, when the Jewish holidays came, they would want to identify themselves. They would say, 'Shin,' the first letter of Shadei, and the other fellow would finish the word and say 'Shadei.' After the Jews left Spain, they used the word 'Shin' as a password, but the Anglo-Saxon who did not understand it called the Jews 'sheeneys.' Whenever you call a Jew a 'sheeney,' you are really blaspheming God."

MOSES AND SELF-MASTERY

"Moses was the adopted son of Pharaoh's daughter. When he saw two Jews fighting, he disapproved and said it was not right, but when he saw an Egyptian fighting a Jew, he killed the Egyptian. Moses lectured in one case and killed in the other. Fearing Pharaoh because he had slain the Egyptian, Moses left civilization and fled into the wilderness.

"These statements about Moses are symbolic—about how a man of unstable temperament can change and develop self-mastery. In the wilderness Moses spent much time meditating. This is symbolized by the bush which was 'burning without being consumed' (Exodus 3:2) and reflected his thoughts: cause and effect, yes and no. This ancient symbolism even persists today in the Orient. They have an expression, 'the brain is on fire.'

"Moses, the apparent weakling, developed self-mastery, after which he returned to Egypt and without fear or hesitation told Pharaoh what to do. By learning self-mastery, Moses was able to carry out the mission of freeing the Jews from slavery, give them the Ten Commandments, and lead them to their own kingdom. He was the chosen messenger of God to carry out this mission, and he succeeded. He did not look for glory or thanks; he did not want temples or monuments built to him. He disappeared from his people and died in an unknown place."

* * *

The following examples show Romano's uniquely practical interpretations of some ancient biblical texts. His illuminating viewpoints seem as applicable to man and his relations to his fellow men today as when they were first recorded.

THE TEN COMMANDMENTS
AFTER NINETY-FIVE YEARS OF LIVING

At the age of ninety-eight, Jacques Romano recorded his own comments on the Ten Commandments.

I. "Thou shalt have no other gods before me."

"There is only one God: This commandment applied then and for all time. When Moses, their leader, disappeared, the people made the golden calf as a substitute for the God of Moses. When Moses returned he combated with this commandment the tendency of the people to revert to idolatry and polytheism. Such practices of polytheism had led historically to corruption and moral decadence."

II. "Thou shalt not make unto thee any graven image, nor any likeness of anything that is in heaven above, or that is in the earth beneath, or that is in the water under the earth: Thou shalt not bow down thyself to them, nor serve them: for I the Lord thy God am a jealous God, visiting the iniquity of the fathers upon the children unto the third and fourth generation of them that hate me; And showing mercy unto thousands of them that love me, and keep my commandments."

"This covers idolatry on land, sea, and in the air. There is only one God. Visiting the iniquity of the fathers upon the children of the third and fourth generation meant the transmission of diseases acquired by dissipation, contamination, and inheritance (syphilis, plague, idiocy, and so forth). I believe that in the Bible sickness was equated with sin. These illnesses were considered to be of mystical origin and were thus understood by the people. For example, 'He did not live a pure life according to the will of God.' The fact is, we do not sin against God as much as we sin against ourselves."

III. "Thou shalt not take the name of the Lord thy God in vain: for the Lord will not hold him guiltless that taketh his name in vain."

"This means, 'do not tell God what to do.' Using God's name promiscuously is disrespectful and belittles Him. It brings God down to man's level. Thus, prayer, which should always be a sincere expression of feeling, can become nothing but a droning phonograph record."

IV. "Remember the Sabbath day, to keep it holy. Six days shalt thou labor, and do all thy work; But the seventh day is the sabbath of the Lord thy God: in it thou shalt not do any work, thou, nor thy son, nor thy daughter, thy manservant, nor thy maidservant, nor thy cattle, nor the stranger that is within thy gates: For in six days the Lord made heaven and earth, the sea and all that in them is, and rested the seventh day: wherefore the Lord blessed the sabbath day, and hallowed it."

"The sabbath day emphasizes that this is God's day. By divorcing himself from his labors, daily chores, and worries, man rests on the sabbath day and strengthens his communion with an infinite influence, the Creator—God. This commandment says, 'Show consideration for human beings and animals.' It provides for rest, and, in turn, leads toward the development of mental and physical self-control. Indirectly it speaks against cruelty to animals."

V. "Honor thy father and thy mother: that thy days may be long upon the land which the Lord thy God giveth thee."

"These early people were not far removed from savagery, incest, and cannibalism. This commandment set up a hierarchy of family rule. It taught them to learn from their parents' experience. It teaches how consideration and affection are learned in the family circle and can be applied to other people outside the family."

VI. "Thou shalt not kill."

"In ancient times when there were disagreements, killing was natural, almost more common than arguing. It is of interest that many people who professed to follow the Ten Commandments subsequently killed people for not accepting them. Contrary to this commandment, they believed might was right. Stronger nations conquered weaker ones; by killing they subjected the people to enslavement and the worship of the conquerors' gods. This commandment marked a signal advance in civilization because it implied that people and nations could disagree with one another and think what they wished but that no physical violence should ever be tolerated."

VII. "Thou shalt not commit adultery."

"This taught respect for family life and possessions. It proscribed breaking up somebody's home."

VIII. "Thou shalt not steal."

"This affirms a man's privilege to own what he has worked for. It means that his possessions and private property must be respected. This, in essence, is the difference between a republican form of government and a fascist or communist form of dictatorship."

IX. "Thou shalt not bear false witness against thy neighbor."

"One should not commit domestic gossip against the other fellow. A gossip is worse than a thief. A thief may steal your purse but not your reputation."

X. "Thou shalt not covet thy neighbor's house, thou shalt not covet thy neighbor's wife, nor his manservant, nor his maidservant, nor his ox, nor his ass, nor anything that is thy neighbor's."

"Do not use false, lying pretenses or suave talk to take advantage of the other fellow's possessions. People who do so have no will power and behave in a greedy, conniving manner. They use tricky methods and pervert the law to appear respectable. But this is only a cloak for their inner hostility and inclination to lie, steal, and cheat."

*   *   *

In the 1920's Romano gave lectures to the artists of the famed Salamagundi Club and the Artists Aid Society dinner in New York. A self-taught artist who originally earned his living in the United States by painting miniature portraits, he applied his highly developed intuitive abilities and research type of mind in drawing his impressions of how he "felt," "saw," and "knew" Jesus and the Betrayer. The following accounts show his singular approach.

CRUCIFIXION—SLOW TORTURE

"The Greek Bible claims that Jesus was crucified on a pole (Greek—*stauros*) and not a cross (Latin—*crux*) as the later Latin translations have it. In some of the early artistic versions of the crucifixion, Jesus was shown standing on a pedestal for public execution. His hands were extended high over His head and nailed or tied to a pole. By being nailed in this way He would not quickly bleed to death, and thus the torture would be prolonged. There are still carvings, paintings, and statues that show Jesus standing on a pedestal.

"In the translation from Greek into Latin, the Romans changed the pole to the cross, and thereby made a more artistic picture, and used an ancient symbol of various meanings. They further embellished this by crossing Jesus's legs and using one nail, instead of one nail for each uncrossed leg as shown in the earlier versions."

THE CONVENTIONAL PICTURES
OF THE MADONNA AND OF JESUS

"In all the paintings of Jesus, His face looks weak and without strength. These pictures of Jesus are based on early Greek physiognomy and phrenology. The early

Greek sculptures of gods and men revealed feminine faces. Even if a beard was put on the face, it was modulated, and there still was no suggestion of strength or character. In classical Greek art, the shape of the head, the forehead, eyes, nose, and chin were all indicated for symmetry and beauty, but not strength.

"In the Christian religion there is the Madonna, and the Madonna was made with a perfect face. According to Greek physiognomy the nose of the Madonna was made perfectly straight to show complete balance of mind. The people who have a nose that is perfectly straight and balanced, however, have never done anything, have never produced a leader. It is the bumpy or irregular nose that is associated with achievement and character.

"The nostril of the Madonna is made small, not too large so as to be in proper proportion. If a nostril is made too large, it indicates boisterousness and deception. If the nostril is too small, according to Greek physiognomy, it shows a limited breathing capacity.

"The upper lip of the Madonna is not long, because that shows mental tenacity and denotes planning ahead. The upper lip of the Madonna is perfectly modulated, because there is nothing for her to plan—everything is planned for her. The upper lip is not made too short, because for a woman this means she is very sensitive and self-conscious.

"The chin of the Madonna was modulated and not too large. A large chin shows determination and impatience, which would not fit the Madonna.

"The forehead of the Madonna was made rounded and bulging. No one seems to understand why, but this was to show that she was innocent. It suggests innocence because all babies have bulging foreheads, and what is more innocent than a baby? As the baby grows up, the forehead becomes flat in the center.

"The eye of the Madonna was made to show modesty, and the eyebrow was made long to show that all the mental propensities were thoroughly developed.

"The head of the Madonna was made perfectly round to show that all the mental faculties were in proper balance. You notice that in all pictures of the Madonna the head looks like a half-circle.

"The hair of the Madonna was made hanging down to show the maiden. Why is this so? Because, according to the Bible, you will find that Rebekah was at the well, and she might have stood there with her hair hanging down, which showed that she was a maiden.

"Now, as it is shown, the head and hair have no spiritual aspect. Hence, in conformity with the ancient Greek precepts they had to bring her shawl in proportion to the hair hanging on the other side, thus forming a triangle and giving the spiritual aspect. This motif was copied from the triangle of the pyramids.

"In order to make the Madonna look superior spiritually, in comparison with just any woman, they gave her a halo, a mark of spirituality. Therefore, it starts to look like a Madonna. Her face and head are perfect.

*   *   *

"Since there cannot be two perfect faces, the classical artists use the Madonna's physiognomy and phrenology in painting the face of Christ. All that I do is raise the eyebrows to show mental agony, sorrow, and grief. I then put a line under the eyes and add the moustache and the beard. Thus, you will find the face of Jesus is nothing but a feminine face with the beard and moustache added."

DA VINCI'S CHRIST

"In order to convince myself that the Renaissance pictures of Christ are feminine, I took da Vinci's famous painting of Jesus with the crown of thorns and noted that the raised position of the head emphasized the feminine nature by prominently displaying the neck. I then photographed the painting, touched out the thorns, put hair in its place and blanked out the moustache and beard. People who viewed the final picture reacted with the question, 'Who is the beautiful lady?'"

THE PORTRAIT OF JESUS BY JACQUES ROMANO

"While I was talking with Margaret Wilson, President Wilson's daughter, who was interested in all kinds of religion (she finally went to India and became a convert to Hindu asceticism), she rebuked me for my criticism of the classical paintings of Christ by the masters. She said, 'If these paintings were so unsatisfactory, why don't you draw a picture of Our Lord in conformity with your interpretations and impressions?' I said, 'Jacques Romano is a realist. Every artist tries to have Jesus look like a native of his country. I have seen sketches where he looked like a Czechoslovakian; and in the warm-climate portraits, Jesus has such a wide nose that he looks like a mulatto. Russian artists once told me that they used an egg for a perfect oval upon which they painted a face. Most of the portraits of Jesus have more resemblance to those diseased and sick people He cured than to Himself.'

"In my drawing, Jesus was a Semite (Jew) and an aristocrat, since through the chain of twenty-six generations, He was descended from King David. Therefore, I had the problem of bringing out the Oriental, Semitic features, His strength of character, and natural healthy aggression, fortitude, and strength. Constantly visualizing a face of humility, representing strength, I followed an urge to draw, and in eighteen minutes the face and message followed.

"Jesus was born in a stable and died on the cross between two thieves. This is symbolic and means that where you were born and died is unimportant. How you live is all important!"

THE PORTRAIT OF THE BETRAYER BY JACQUES ROMANO

"From the Scriptures I could deduce that Judas was charming and likable. He was treasurer and possibly a leader among the other eleven apostles. There must have been something fascinating and trustworthy about his expression. If I am to portray a great statesman and organizer, this aspect must be compromised, because Judas betrayed his Master. His physiognomy must be spoiled in such a way that he will look like a villain, but not like an ordinary villain. Therefore, in order to please the multitudes I distorted his face and gave him a conniving expression and cynical smile."

DA VINCI'S JUDAS

"In his famous painting of the Last Supper, da Vinci used different Italian countrymen as models for Christ and the disciples. For instance, a gentle monk posed for Christ.

However, da Vinci had trouble finding a suitable subject to pose for Judas. He went to the dungeons and found many criminals who were quite unsuitable. Finally, he found his model. He looked at the man very carefully, and later, while making the painting, he discovered that this same man who posed for Judas was originally his model for Christ in one of his previous portraits. The subject told da Vinci that after sitting for the earlier paintings of Jesus he was royally treated by various noble Italian families and that this activity led to dissipation and ruin and finally his commission as a model for the painting of Judas by the unsuspecting da Vinci."

*   *   *

Recalling an incident of his childhood, Romano once said, "When I heard the parable about Jesus driving the devils into the swine and their rushing headlong down the precipice to drown, I asked the priest why the pigs should suffer, since they had nothing to do with the devils. Feigning innocence, I asked if the pigs were used as sinkers." Romano's interest in parables continued throughout his life, although not perhaps with the same youthful levity. He felt that the world's greatest source of knowledge is to be found in the parables of the ancients. The following illustrations reflect this opinion.

PARABLES

"In order to obtain knowledge I educated myself in how to think and reason things out. For instance, why should I read a book of two or three hundred pages, full of vocabulary, but possibly of little significance? Consequently, I began to read parables, and then I found a

particular parable that interested me. Compressed in only
two lines were wisdom and meaning. How much that man
knew worldly affairs to condense it into only two lines!
When I find a parable it is as though 'I've heard it before,
and I am trying to recall it.'

"Of all the great philosophers who spoke in parables
none had a college education. They were sensitive to conditions. They did not have a rich vocabulary; they said
what they meant. The parables illustrated what they felt.
I give people parables to clarify what I am thinking. On
occasion they have turned to old Hindu or other writings
and found the parables I quoted. Because I had no formal
education I just sense these things."

EYE FOR (AN) EYE

" 'Eye for (an) eye—tooth for (a) tooth' (Exodus 21:24)
really means eye *under* an eye, coming from the Hebrew
word 'tachas' meaning 'under, being subservient.' Place
yourself in the other fellow's position: How would you
like your own eye knocked out before you knocked the
other fellow's eye out? The Gentiles could not understand
the symbol of an eye under an eye, and, accordingly, incorrectly interpreted the ancient Hebrew symbols in a
hostile, vile way, discrediting the Ten Commandments,
which preached moderation and nonviolence. The Gentiles exacted a sadistic penalty of an eye for an eye."

WHEN TO TALK

"King Solomon said that 'even a fool, when he holdeth
his peace, is counted wise; when he shutteth his lips he is
esteemed as prudent' (Proverbs 17:28). When should one

talk? A personal experience solved this proverb for me.

"Many years ago when I was in England, I loved to roam and visit off-the-beaten-path places. One day I entered a pub and ordered a glass of beer to be sociable. While I was leaning against the bar, an Englishman asked if I were a foreigner, and I said, 'Yes.' 'How do you like our country compared to the United States?' he asked, and I answered, 'I am very sensitive to surroundings. I have found something here I could not find in the whole United States. Every step I take brings me into new contacts with invisible vibrations of your past history, and they seem to affect my subconscious. Gradually, I am consciously becoming aware of your country's history.'

"We talked about these things until I noticed a little commotion; the men in the pub started to turn away from me. I overheard one of the men in a distant corner say to his friend, 'I think this fellow is cracked.' They were not acquainted with the vocabulary I was using, so I left the pub and continued my wanderings.

"Later, I entered a small restaurant. The place was unpretentious in every way. I spotted an elderly gentleman sitting alone, and asked if I could sit at his table. He was having milk and crackers. He said, 'You are a stranger here, aren't you?' I said, 'Yes.' He asked, 'You are a foreigner?' 'Yes.' 'How does England compare with your country, the United States, I assume?'

"I began to say that England has a superior history and that when in his country, in my every step, I am able to feel the conditions of more than one thousand years of great history. Then, I gradually drifted to my opinion that when we are sensitive we can feel conditions of the past in the air we breathe and the ground we tramp upon. Whatever I said he agreed with and commented, 'Yes, it's possible.' I kept on talking more and more, but all he said was, 'Yes, I agree. You're right. We are creatures who are able to sense things.'

"Then I was through and said goodbye. He bade me farewell, and I left. I was so glad to have had the chance to talk with him and tell him about my feelings for England. When I paid the bill I told the proprietor how much I enjoyed sitting with the 'kindly old gentleman who was so congenial and pleasant.' The proprietor looked at me and said, 'Yes, he is that kind of a man. Do you know who he is?' I said, 'No. Who?' 'He is Professor MacDonald, who wrote twelve volumes on the philosophy of life. He is considered to be one of our most famous philosophers.'

"I had made a fool of myself. Then I remembered King Solomon's proverb. I had learned when to talk. Let the other fellow talk first; then I'll know whether to keep my mouth shut or not."

TURN THE CHEEK

" 'Turn the other cheek' (Matthew 5:39) means that if someone slapped me on the left cheek I should turn the right cheek. I must have acted wrongly to have provoked him to slap me in the face. To turn to him the other cheek means to apologize to him for bringing on that condition. This is borne out by the fact that in the Hebrew language there is no word for apology. But to turn the right cheek is symbolic of the act of apologizing."

GIVING

" 'Let not thy left hand know what the right hand doeth' (Matthew 6:3). If you are kind to anyone and try to help him, it should be a natural reaction. Consequently, do not look for any thanks from the one you help, because he only tells you how miserable and unhappy he is. He only gives you his unhappiness in return for the kindness that you gave him. It means, if you are really generous and help somebody, you should not have to crow about it. If you help him from the motive of receiving thanks, you'll suffer for every charitable act. If you give, it should be for the good it does you. If you give to be glorified, you will be disappointed and never find happiness."

DO NOT CAST PEARLS TO THE SWINE

" 'Neither cast your pearls before the swine' (Matthew 7:6) means when to talk and when not to talk. Pearls are symbolic of wisdom. No matter how you turn a pearl it is always the same. In any language wisdom is always the same.

"The pig is supposed to be a dumb animal, because any animal that you call will turn his head and look at you. The pig does not. But pigs are, in fact, the smartest herbivorous animals. Because of its particular anatomy the pig cannot completely turn its head as other animals do. This parable teaches us that, if you have anything to say of wisdom, be sure the one you are talking to looks at you. Do not waste your wisdom on someone who does not look at you when you talk to him."

BUDDHA

"Buddha existed six hundred years before Jesus. He was a prince, the son of a great king; and he showed much

character. He was married early in youth and they had a
child. He would ask the slaves questions and then sneak
out to the marketplace, where he noted the injustices of
life. He taught people righteousness and love. The Devil
said that if Buddha went out any more, he would enter
his palace and destroy his wife and baby. But, Buddha,
despite the threat, went out and gathered twelve disciples
and traveled from place to place preaching his religion.
He found kindness and beauty in everything.

"Buddha and his disciples were traveling along the road
one day when they came upon the carcass of a dog. Each of
the disciples carefully walked away from the dog and commented on the degeneration and stench. Finally, Buddha
came and opened the beast's mouth and said, 'What
beautiful teeth the animal has.' "

ABDUL BAHA

"Abdul Baha was a friendly, sincere man working for
humanity. He had great understanding. He said, 'Live up
to your religion.' He taught kindness, consideration, and
honesty. Like Jesus who taught 'go out and preach, but
do not kill,' Abdul Baha said, 'Do not judge one by what
he was baptized, but by his actions.'

"Abdul Baha was dressed in simple, plain clothes and
wore a turban. He wanted a universal language. He was
married and had a family. For a long time the Turks kept
him in jail. I met him when he had just gotten out of jail,
in Syria. He would say, 'Well, let us break bread and salt
together.'

"Abdul Baha was beloved by everyone who met him.
He was not interested in miracles, psychic phenomena, or
hairsplitting theological controversies. Bahā u llāh, his

father, was the forerunner and prophesied that his son would be a great man.

"Abdul Baha was one of the most spiritual men I ever met. He had an understanding of human strength and weakness. When a Roman Catholic came to him, he would quote some verse from Catholic sources and say, 'Son, if you live up to these Scriptures, you also belong to the Brotherhood of the Bahai. We say that all who follow the teachings of their faiths should be brothers; there should be no hate between different faiths and nationalities.' Abdul Baha used quotations from Mohammedan, Hebrew, and various Christian sources to illustrate the brotherhood of mankind.

"Once at a feast in the Orient they were eating roast lamb, but there was a fellow who would not eat, and appeared to be ill at ease. He walked around in a hesitating manner and did not know how to act in a crowd. Abdul realized that he lacked confidence and was not at home, so he gently hit him with a cane and said, 'Brother, come on with me.' He took him by the arm and said, 'Let us eat together.' One of the guests later remarked, 'Master why did you strike this man with your cane? Wasn't that hard on the poor fellow?' 'No, he wanted to eat and was afraid. He would not understand the language of a kind approach, so I gently touched him with my cane and smiled; this way he learned that I was friendly.' "

THE TRAMP'S REWARD

"I had been six months in the United States and was flat broke. My clothes were shabby and food was hard to come by. To all appearances I was a tramp. One cold, blustery evening I noticed a well-dressed man in a tall silk hat, Prince Albert coat, and diamond stickpin, in the company of an elegant woman in evening dress. While the couple were turning the corner on Fifth Avenue, the lady dropped her purse. I grabbed it and edged up to the woman and said, 'I beg your pardon, Madam—' but before I could say another word the fellow hit me on the head with his cane. Blood trickled down my face. I said, 'I beg your pardon, Sir. The lady lost her purse and I want to give it back to her.' I handed her the purse, 'There it is.'

"He said, 'Oh, I'm dreadfully sorry,' and he put his hand in his pocket, took out some bills, and gave them to me.

"'I beg your pardon,' I said, 'I'm not looking for charity, but for some work. I'm awfully sorry this happened. Don't worry about it, there is a certain law that governs everything.'

"I walked down the street and said to myself, 'I can't understand: I want to do the right thing, and I get struck on the head.' That bothered me. Why should I get hit on the head when I had goodness in my heart and tried to do the right thing? I walked down to Union Square and sat on a bench where I spent my nights. On the third day, it dawned on me. 'I know why he hit me on the head. My prayers were wrong. My prayers to God were to find some money, and, if I found money, it meant that someone would have to have lost it and consequently suffer. Now, I know why I was struck on the head. I deserved more than that!'

"About two weeks after this experience I met a man who looked like an Oriental. He quietly nodded to me and gave me a peculiar sign with his hand. I'd seen this a long time ago, but it did not register. The man said, 'Well, now you are thinking, and thinking will make you happy in all your future days, whether you are in financial need or not. Now you understand why you were hit on the head.' This man was an Essene on his way to the Orient. The Essenes are all over the world, but they never identify themselves. They never invite you to become an Essene; they have no policy to be good, because for an Essene it is just a case of righteousness. The story of Job is symbolic of how a man is initiated into the Essenes. Such a man knows he is being initiated. If he has to be sworn to secrecy, that is no good, and he will never be able to become an Essene. As shown in the story of Job, no matter what happens, it is always for the best, and there is a reason for it. Just like my being hit with the cane."

THE SERPENT

"In the Orient the serpent is symbolic of wisdom. While sitting in the desert one day, I wondered why this was so. Soon a snake writhed along the sand. He looked at me, shook his head and said, 'You here? You do not know how to get along in this world? You worry? Look at me. They call me "wisdom." Do you know why? You walk straight, with your head to the sky and your feet on the ground. You speak several languages. You can cry for pain, help, and joy. You have hands strong enough to pick something up in them. You are always looking down on everything. Look at me, I crawl on my belly, I have no hands and feet, no voice, and I am getting along nicely. Look at my skin. Am I not healthy? I am under the feet of everyone that can step on me and kill me. As a serpent, I am in a worse position than anyone in the world. Yet I get along beautifully, and I am healthy. And that's why they call me "wisdom." ' "

THE BEAR

"Two old friends went bear hunting. One was attacked by a huge brown bear, which sprang from behind a tree and seized the hunter and squeezed him in his powerful forelegs. The second hunter acted quickly and saved his friend by shooting the bear. When the first hunter freed himself from the death hug, he shouted, 'Look at the hole you made. You spoiled the fur.' "

DOG AND CAT

"There are three sides to a story—your side, my side, and the side I do not know. Therefore, I never make a positive statement. If you disagree with me, give me a chance and I will prove you are right. If you condemn a man, you do it according to your own standards.

"I learned much from animals. Once a dog was given to me. I already had a cat. In the beginning they were always howling and fighting. Later on they ate and slept together; they seemed wonderful friends. I asked the cat, 'How come you don't argue and fight any more?' The cat said, in his own way, that is, with an independent air, 'We understand each other.' I said, 'Well, people understand each other like sweethearts do before marriage. Yet there are arguments.' And the cat answered, 'You know, it took me some time to find out that he's a dog, and I'm a cat. I, as a cat, never try to make a dog meow, but let him bark; so we don't argue.' "

CHARITY

"A poor man was standing in front of a building and eating grass. The owner came out and said, 'What are you doing?' The man said, 'I'm hungry and starved.' The owner said, 'Why don't you go into the backyard; the grass is longer there.'

"True kindness and charity are like this: A man came to the door and said he was hungry and wished bread. He was told to go to the kitchen in the back of the house. This is not charity. True charity is when a man knocks on the door and you say, 'Oh, I myself was just going to eat. Please come in and join me.' That is what my father did."

"IF I HAD A MILLION DOLLARS"

Jacques Romano was a man who never had more than a thousand dollars in the bank at any time during his life. He often said he had been broke but never poor. Once, near the end of his long life and in desperate need of money, he received a call from a leading New York bank informing him (using his proper name and address) that he had been given ten thousand dollars by someone in Montevideo, Uruguay. To the surprise and consternation of his friends and the bank, Romano said there was a mistake. He refused the money, telling the bank they were in error. His friends were shocked and convinced he must have taken leave of his senses. But within a week, the bank official phoned to say his face was red and he was grateful to Romano, who had saved his job. For what had seemed so accurate was wrong. At the age of ninety-eight and a half Romano had been proved entirely correct.

One day his wife Molly said to him, "I wish I had a million dollars." Jacques asked, "What would you do with a million dollars?"

"I would like to help the poor and the sick."

"Molly, if that is what you want, then God will never give you a million dollars."

"Why shouldn't God give it to me? I mean well and I'd give every cent to charity."

"Molly, do you know what your prayer is? It's a selfish, mean prayer, and God will never listen to you. Do you want to have people made sick for the purpose of your giving them a million dollars? Do you want to bring on all this misery so that you can show off and have everyone know how well you can help? You do not have to pray for help, because God knows it."

VII

HOW TO HOLD AN AUDIENCE IN THE PALM OF YOUR HAND

"The intelligentsia are those who spend other people's money."

FOR over sixty years Jacques Romano was in demand as an after-dinner speaker. His friends and various newspaper clippings bear witness to his impact on an audience. The credible-incredible man spoke to service clubs, chambers of commerce, educators, and others. For example, in 1912, with Dr. J. Bentley Squires, he spoke at a benefit banquet for St. Luke's Hospital, in New York City. He often appeared at the Explorer's Club. He spoke to college and alumni groups at Yale, Princeton, University of Pennsylvania, Columbia, Lafayette, and elsewhere. His inimitable style and rapid-fire delivery left people amazed and breathless. This pattern of making the phenomenal believable continued almost to the end of his life, when he squeezed in lectures at Sierra State University in Los Angeles, the New York Psychology Forum, the Wisconsin Organic Club at Manitowoc, and a talk on "Yogi and Health" at the Waldorf-Astoria with Madame Devi. When he was ninety-seven he went on a Grace Line Caribbean cruise sponsored by the New York Academy of Medicine and participated in scholarly lectures on sex. This brief summary omits the innumerable church and social groups he lectured to. He celebrated his ninety-eighth birthday by giving a noontime half-hour interview on radio station WNCN-FM, New York.

Since Romano was so different from anyone else and was able to do so many extraordinary things, it would not have been surprising if he had had considerable ego. Yet Romano was personally quite modest. He had the spirit of true humility. Others wrote his lecture handbills, which used such phrases as "the greatest man of our age"—"an amazing man with amazing powers and ability"—"delving into the incredible"—"the enigma of a century"—"the most bewildering, the most baffling"—"miracles or mysteries."

Many physicians, with their wives and families, were invited to after-dinner parties to meet Romano. When they were told on the telephone that the guest of honor was a nonagenarian, the would-be guests cleared their throats and hoped to be delivered from an evening of boredom with "some old fool prattling on and on." But by the time the evening was in full swing, most of the guests were completely charmed and gave rapt attention to the spellbinding Romano. Some few may have professed disbelief, but no one ever fell asleep. At a deeper level, others were genuinely impressed by the fact that Romano could—and did—"read their minds." The session often stretched from 7:30 P.M. until 2:00 A.M., but almost no one was tired. At least Jacques Romano, who seemed to draw energy out of his audience, never looked tired. He was still going strong.

Rian James's 1931 newspaper column "Reverting to

Type" was still a good description of Romano in 1960—
except for the color of the eyeglass frames:

"Pry away a few hundred people from the outer fringe
of a human circle at a night club, a Park Avenue apartment, or a Sutton Place mansion, and the dark, nervous,
tortoise-shelled little individual with the agile hands, the
beaming face, and the hypnotic voice that you'll find
in its center is Jacques Romano. We'll bet on it."

The following excerpts give some idea of how Romano
held his audience. He had something to say to everyone—
lawyers, salesmen, educators, housewives.

LAWYERS

Speaking before the New York Bar Association, Romano
said: "Gentlemen, I am honored to talk to you. When I
received this invitation I was really quite frightened. I
am familiar with medical things and have spoken to physicians many times, but never to lawyers. So, in desperation,
I went to an old retired lawyer friend of mine for advice.
The old judge said, 'Calm yourself, young man. Lawyers
are the best, most understanding and versatile of people.
They can adapt themselves to both sides. Now, if you go
to a doctor and you have gangrene, there is no argument.
The doctor tells you that he has to cut off the leg and
that's it. But take a lawyer; he has a philosophy of life.
After listening a short while to a crook, he can make him
appear as such an honest man! And he can take an innocent man and make him appear as such a hypocrite that
the jury will laugh! It all depends on who engages the
lawyer first.'

"I used to write Christmas cards for a millionaire in his own handwriting. Once in a Norristown court trial, at the turn of the century, a son claimed the estate of his mother after her death. The son claimed that his mother had given him a check for $500 before she died. A lady relative contested this, saying that the check was not made out in the mother's handwriting. They called me as an expert and asked if I knew whether the check was really in the deceased mother's handwriting. I said 'Yes! The court should ask the complaining relative if she knew the deceased's handwriting.' She insisted that she did. I then had her write her name three times and, before the judge, I forged her name three times. We marked on the backs of the papers which I had forged. They were then mixed up and the complaining relative picked three from the six, two of which were mine, as her own handwriting. The case was settled in favor of the son. The check was valid. The relative should not have set herself up as an expert.

"Another example happened in a small town. The signature on a check was contested. I was paid as an expert witness. In order to win the case, I made a photographic enlargement of the handwriting on the check, which showed the relaxations and impressions of the pen. The writing was not as emphatic as the other samples of the writing. I said, 'Your Honor, it depends on when it was written, and if a blotter was used or not.' I wrote my name several times and blotted some of the samples, so that the light and dark shades of the inking were obscured. The case was dismissed and the check was declared legitimate.

"In 1903 I was in the English Hotel in Indianapolis, Indiana. I showed the clerk how I could do crooked work with cards and forgery. I forged a whole page of the hotel register. Two men who were watching me came over and asked if I wanted to make some extra money. They wanted to give me bonds to sign for a man who was supposed to have died. They asked me to sign two hundred of them for $2,000. I said, 'I'm sorry, but I'm subject to horrible attacks of writer's cramp.'"

CRIMINALS

"The study of criminals has always interested me. Years ago on the Bowery, I was invited to parties thrown by pickpockets, confidence men, and perhaps some murderers. Because I was careful to refrain from calling them crooks or to lecture them they respected me. They were a superstitious lot. Some of them wore a rabbit's foot or carried charms, medallions, and lucky pieces. Many had taboos, such as walking under a ladder or letting a black cat cross their path. Many believed in numerology, astrology, and palm reading.

"They had a strange code of honor. Each crook tried to show how he was personally constructive in managing his own affairs, while he criticized the antisocial and depraved conduct of the other criminals. There was 'Jimmy the Grip,' whose specialty was to work only in hotels. He was a gentleman thief who hung around hotel lobbies until he spotted a likely victim. Sometimes he would just pick up a grip or two and calmly walk out. Or he would modify his techniques and give an obliging bellhop a quarter with instructions to buy him a cigar. That was all the time that Jimmy would need. He was 'so honest' that when he went to Harry's 'fence,' he would patiently and quietly look out the window at the street below while, behind Jimmy's back, Harry opened the grips and examined the just-pilfered loot.

"One party I shall never forget hinged on the superstitious faith of the criminals. I hypnotized a confidence woman and by suggestion made her a medium. While she was deeply entranced, I looked around the room and finally picked Joey the crook, a seventeen-year-old, sallow, undernourished-appearing boy. I said, 'Joey, is your mother dead?' He nodded his head, 'Yes.' 'Now, I want you to take hold of this woman's hand.' Then I asked, 'Would you like to get a message from your mother?' He softly choked, 'Yes.' When the woman was deeply under my spell, her voice suddenly changed and she said, 'Joey, are you there? This is your mother. How I used to send you to church and how happy I was when you would come home from church and your behavior was so nice and lovely! But now, for the past few years, since my departure, you have changed, and I have no rest or peace. How my soul suffers. You are destroying your life. Please go back to church, be a good boy, and give peace to my soul.'

"Upon hearing these words, Joey began to cry. He held the 'medium's' hand tighter and tighter. At the climax I made the woman's head drop to her chest, and she breathed more and more heavily. I glanced around the room and saw tears in the eyes of many. Joey got down on his knees and kissed the woman's hand. Everyone was numb and perfectly quiet.

"Many years later I learned how Joey had reformed and from that evening on had led an honorable life. The immediate reaction of the group was interesting. Many of the crooks wanted to talk to me privately. They told me how careful and selective they were in their crimes to see that no one was ever really hurt. One crook said he only 'stole insured things, like silks, silver, diamonds, and furs.' Another one robbed old people, 'who only had heirlooms and lived in the past.' One avoided 'young people, because what little they had was closely connected with love and romance.' One thief, in and out of jail for eleven years, indignantly protested his moral innocence: 'I'm honest, I'm no crook. I steal directly and not indirectly. Why, I am different—I stick my hand in the pocket and then take the money out. A gambler cheats by signals and the like in an open game with many witnesses, and he is protected by the police.'

"I pondered over some of these experiences and wondered if an abused system of justice does not stimulate dishonesty. So many criminals said, 'If I had plenty of money and a good lawyer, I could always get out. I can appeal and appeal until I die a natural death, not hungry, and not in jail!' "

A SALESMAN WITH PERSONAL MAGNETISM

In the 1920's Romano used to lecture the sales executives of the Melville Shoe Company (Thom McAn shoes). His practical suggestions included these:

"When you meet a customer, speak in a mellow tone. But if he speaks loudly, don't talk in a mellow tone because he will think you are a sissy. Raise your voice strongly. A positive attitude is the only convincing attitude. Doubt, fear, hesitancy, inaccuracy, and uncertainty should all be classed as business sins. Their punishment should be failure. The salesmen who would succeed should be clean, clear, positive, convincing, sure of his goods, and sure of himself. Armed with these qualifications, failure is impossible.

"If a potential customer sits with his legs crossed and shakes his foot, don't make your sentences long. Cut them short, because the customer is restless and impatient. Hold the article you are selling a little higher than his nose, so he cannot think. Know your subject well: how to praise it and how to knock it. You must understand all the pros and cons. Never talk to a man when his hands are clasped. He might feel threatened and is in a state of self-preservation and on the defensive. He will be a hard customer to convince.

"For example, when talking to the potential customer, I might say that a friend just sent me some Cuban cigars and ask him if he'd like to taste one. When the customer opens his hands, he may be more approachable. When I see him walk, I can also tell the kind of man he is; whether he is shifty, has trouble concentrating, is aggressive or shy. If he closes his fist with the thumb over the fingers when he thinks, it means that he does not want to buy anything, and he means exactly what he says, no more, no less. If the thumb is inside, I know that he is undecided. If he swears and is restless, I say 'Well, let's go out and have a glass of beer.'

"No businessman can be truthfully classed as a success unless he can look his own soul in the face and shake hands with his conscience."

"There is no such thing as will power, it is stubbornness."

"If you are conscious of doing work, you tire and must rest. I am not conscious of work; therefore I never tire."

ENLIVEN YOUR CONVERSATION

As a supersalesman Romano was a paradox. He could have achieved the heights of material success by his abilities and brains; yet he turned away and used his abilities for other purposes. Dr. Wanderman once recalled how Romano befriended one of America's leading financiers by being his personal healer and by entertaining the tycoon's customers with his sprightly repartee, psychic works, and lively cartoons four to five nights a week. Yet Romano never took a cent—nor was anything ever offered! Once when Romano's tiny Jamol Company was in trouble and needed a little money, the same tycoon refused to lend as much as a dime.

"By knowing how to improvise, you enliven your repartee under all sorts of conditions. As an example, never prepare how you are going to talk business with another person. Do not memorize your points, since this can become too rigid, cramp your style, and make your presentation ineffective. Study the man's general attitude and reactions. Adjust your answers to his questions in a logical fashion that is understandable to the man with a point of view contrary to your own.

"In order to demonstrate this faculty of adaptive perception, I have people draw a crooked line an inch and a half to two inches long. Instead of saying that this line is a completely meaningless scribble, I claim that there is something in it. I would tell the man beforehand that I could see eight distinct faces in this crooked line. The artists at the Salamagundi Club always enjoyed this stunt."

THE GREAT DEPRESSION
Newspaper interview with L. L. Stevenson,
Detroit News—1930

" 'Present conditions,' Romano said, 'are not a depression. They are merely a readjustment.' Had he money to invest, he declared, he would buy four things. First, food, because people must always eat. Second, medicines, because people worry themselves into illness. Third, he would invest heavily in cosmetics. Of all, cosmetics, he held, are the best investment, because woman, in good times or bad, persists in beautifying herself. So involved did the cosmetics discussion get that we never learned the fourth commodity."

"I NEVER HAD A CHANCE"

"Menshikov teaches society women the correct posture in a riding academy in Long Island. He told me that he was a Russian nobleman and that his father owned more than twenty-five square miles of land before the Bolshevik revolution exiled the family. He said, 'My father was very rich, had huge estates, servants, and art treasures. I had nothing to do, and I never received any formal education. You see, I never had a chance.'

"The garage man at Greenwood Lake was strikingly handsome. His profile looked like John Barrymore's. I asked him how, with his good looks and appearance, he was struggling for a living in a greasy, damp garage. It seemed to be quite a contradiction. He looked up, paused and said, 'My parents were very poor and I didn't have an education. This is all I can do. You see, I never had a chance.' "

AFTER-DINNER ROMANOISMS

"Education is like religion, but religion does not teach you how to think and to deny things—only to accept."

"Education is a profession; intelligence seeks the third side of the story."

"Education tends to retard the process of observation."

"That which annoys us is our master. Dislikes were my teachers."

"Understand your dislikes; they will teach you cause and effect."

"Miracles are just nature's law."

"If you say something once, and the one you are talking to does not understand, talk about the weather."

"A question is a concentrated form of a confession."

"Wishful thinking is a mental narcotic that stimulates procrastination."

"Genius is nothing but a narrow escape from being an imbecile."

"Do you seek knowledge or are you inquisitive? Some people keep their windows clean to get more light; others wash their windows so they can better look into their neighbor's private home."

"Pictures I did not like made me an art critic."

"To know thyself means to understand yourself by realizing your abilities in your life work. This will help you discard mentally obstructing air bubbles. Be a realist; do not expect to illuminate reality with Aladdin's lamp."

"Understanding eliminates our three enemies—fear, worry, and hate."

"With love and understanding there is no loneliness."

"There is a difference between thinking and reading."

"Mr. Romano, I understand you had no formal education; how did you acquire so much knowledge?" "I was not educated to memorize, I was born to analyze and observe."

"Lecturing a child is a waste of time. You might as well talk to a dead person. But standing in a corner where you cannot jump, the body will affect the mind and the child will learn discipline."

"To be ignorant of one's ignorance is a malady of ignorance. To ignore is a sign that we still suffer irritation."

"Tomorrow I hope to realize how little I know today."

[To a college graduating class]: "Gentlemen, save your diplomas; for Heaven's sakes don't lose them, or you'll have nothing to prove you are educated!"

"A fatalist is one who lost or never understood the law of self-preservation; how to avoid danger and recognize safety. Mosquitoes have no sense of self-preservation."

"Tradition is based on gossip."

"I'd rather be called stupid and say something sensible once in a while, than talk stupidity and make a fool of myself."

"Don't judge me or anyone else by yourself because of your own mental attitude."

"I've yet to find a fool. When you compare him to yourself he's a fool. Can you argue with a color-blinded man about red and green?"

"It takes me exactly three minutes to read the news-papers. I look at the headlines and then make up my own lies."

"Anyone with a vocabulary of more than eight hundred words can run for the U.S. Senate."

*   *   *

Despite having met and performed for most of the élite of his day, Romano remained unaffected. A biographer recalls how Romano used to run through his daily mail, and after reading the letters, casually toss them in the wastebasket. An autograph collector would have been sorely frustrated. Just to illustrate, one item saved from the incinerator concerned one of America's leading politi-cians. He was the master-mind and boss of one of the country's most notorious machines. This man was a "presi-dent-maker"* and had as part of his fiefdom an enormous top-heavy medical-center complex that fueled his power base with votes and jobs, both real and imaginary. Al-though the "friend of the poor" had become a multimil-lionaire and had at his call vast numbers of distinguished physicians with their impressive professorial portfolios, the man's wife was the patient of Jacques Romano. This sort of situation was not an isolated one. Other examples involved many leading world figures: lay, professional, and clerical.

MARK TWAIN

"At heart, Mark Twain was one of the saddest men I ever met. Many times a person has to play a part in life.

---

* FDR, after having a personal demonstration, gave Jacques Romano an autographed photograph.

For Mark Twain humor was an outlet to cover up his inner self so that people would not know what he was really like. When I read his Joan of Arc, I felt that he was very depressed. Once after he moved out, I went to his Fifth Avenue apartment, and the walls seemed to reek of melancholy."

MAHATMA GANDHI

"I met Gandhi when he was practicing law in Africa. At that time, he was an Episcopalian, and he loved to wear a high silk hat and Prince Albert coat, which looked rather odd on him. Later, he gave up the practice of law and his Western customs to return to India. Not being a violent man, he advocated passive resistance, which was suitable to the nonaggressive nature of many Hindus. There was no fight (as commonly understood in Western countries) in the Mahatma's nature. With his policies and frequent fasts, he baffled the British Lion and, almost singlehandedly, brought an empire to its knees."

EDISON

Dr. Seymour S. Wanderman recalls how Romano, an excellent practical chemist and inventor, was well known to such scientists as Millikan, Pupin, and Einstein. On numerous occasions Romano also performed before Edison, Burroughs, Henry Ford, and Harvey Firestone.

Once Romano recalled: "Edison slept only four hours a day but, for another four hours in his office, he was completely undisturbed and thinking. He was interested in psychic phenomena and mysticism. He and Luther Burbank were great friends. When I met Edison he asked if I had any system in my chemical research, and I said, 'No, I just get a feeling and then do it.' He quipped, 'Well, I take the chemicals, put them together and do not know what will happen, but as long as they do not explode, I am satisfied.' He then said, 'I understand you are a psychic.' I told him that I never claimed this, but I then proceeded to show him a stunt that Professor Reese had performed for him and greatly impressed him with. Reese had a member of the audience write a message on a piece of paper which he then folded up in his hand. Reese later took the paper and held it to his forehead in order to 'concentrate.' After this, he returned the paper to its author and ordered him to burn it. After the ashes were rolled away he proceeded to astound his audience by telling the exact message. I did the same trick for Edison, which was based on distraction and the substitution of papers by sleight of hand."

CHRISTOPHER COLUMBUS

Often the audience would be astounded by what Romano said. It just couldn't be so. Although it was impossible to check on all his many experiences, spot checks of much of the material never failed to verify them, or at least indicate the need for more study. In no instance was he ever flatly contradicted, taking into account the surrounding factors and times. Whether it was apocryphal in part, or not at all, this gem about Christopher Columbus comes to mind.

Jacques Romano
shortly after
coming to the
United States

Profile of
Jacques Romano,
age 25, in 1889—

Moreno & Lopez
Photographers

Romano, 1891, about
twenty-seven years old

With a beautiful companion before the turn of the century

Jacques Romano: A toreador for charity, about 1900

Jacques Romano at the age of about thirty-five, 1899

Lecture at St. Luke's Hospital benefit,
New York City, about 1912, age 48.

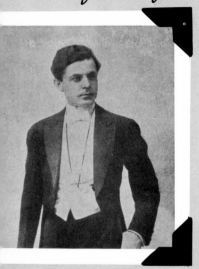

With a senorita
about 1900

Jacques Romano's
wedding photograph,
1914, age 50

December 24th/08
Ed. Williman

Card feats at the home of
the President of Uruguay, 1908

Jacques and
Molly
Romano,
1915

Jacques Romano
at the age
of seventy

Jacques
Romano
at the
age of
eighty-one

To an understanding
friend Dr. D.E. Schwartz
Jacques Romano Mar 30 - 1958

Jacques Romano in 1958 at the age of ninety-four

Jacques Romano in 1959 at the age of ninety-five

Jacques Romano in 1961 at the age of ninety-seven

Jacques Romano at the age of ninety-eight

Jacques Romano's handwriting at the end of his life.

JAMOL CO. - Specialists in Iodine Products
101 MAIDEN LANE · · NEW YORK 38, N. Y.
BOwling Green 9-7488

March 8 1958

Dear Dr Schwarz

To write for the sake of exposing my handwriting is like being my own lawyer to prosecute and defend at the same time.

My handwriting is to represent me by proxy before the judge. The best I can do is to quote some conclusions which are entwined with daily economics and future realization.

Three thing make the superman, a fertile mind, a deep understanding and a cultivated taste to be able to think streight. Streight thinking is the fruit of reason

as ever   Jacques Romano

"As a child, I remember how it was common knowledge, among the Spanish prelates, that Christopher Columbus was neither of Genoese nor of Spanish origin, but was a Christian convert of Hebrew antecedents. Columbus studied navigation in Genoa. When the Spanish disclaimed him, he was immediately accepted by the Italians. However, there is no conclusive proof that he was born in Italy, and in all his letters he never used the Italian language, but Spanish. Years later, in New York, I met a Jewish Turk, by name Nahoum, who claimed to be related to Columbus, and who told me the same thing. Also, William Randolph Hearst once sent two reporters to Spain who returned with documents from Jesuit sources and the Spanish government, which showed this to be true. The hypothesis has also been subscribed to by the famous Spanish historian, Salvador de Madariaga. It helps to explain why a man who discovered a new world and brought great wealth to an empire could be put in chains and brought home to die in a dungeon.

"As I originally heard the story from Nahoum, Christopher (the Cross Bearer) Columbus's real name was Mordecai Ben Chaim de Monterosa. Monterosa was a common Spanish Jewish name, similar to the German name Rosenberg. An outstanding Jew associated with Columbus was Don Abarbanel, one of the chief rabbis, and also a physician to Queen Isabella. It is ironic that the Jews were expelled from Spain the same year that Columbus discovered America, 1492. Don Abarbanel chose to leave Spain with his people. Queen Isabella, who offered him the sanctuary and privilege of her court, was surprised when Don Abarbanel spurned her aid. When confronting the man who chose exile with his people rather than high position and state honors, she asked, 'And not you too?' Upon leaving the country, legend maintains, Don Abarbanel pronounced a curse on Spain: 'Spain will be punished by God, Spain will lose her power and be conquered by other nations for the abuse she gave the Jews.'

"Other prominent Jews in Spain were Raquel de Moniz, Queen Isabella's first lady-in-waiting; Beatriz Enriquez, who may also have been of Jewish origin, the mother of Columbus's natural son, Fernando; and Luis de San Angel, a wealthy influential Spanish Jew, who was instrumental in getting financial support for the Columbus expedition. The Jews had the hope of finding another country where they would be free from the persecution of the Inquisition. Most of Columbus' sailors, who did not mutiny, were Jews; and Gonzales, who first put the Spanish flag on Santo Domingo, was a Jewish physician.

"Columbus frequently used Hebrew scriptural allusions in his writings. His signature, as it appeared in triangular form on letters and documents, was a mystery:

S. A. S.
X. M. Y.
X. p. o. ferens

However, these symbols are intelligible when translated into an ancient Hebrew prayer for forgiveness:

Shadai
Shadai Adonoy Shadai
Yehova Molai Chesed
Nauthai ovon, pesha chatuo

By using this secret way of signing letters, Columbus alluded to the faith of his fathers while, with the zeal often ascribed to a convert, he added new possessions to the Holy Catholic Spanish Crown. There is still much mystery about the 'Lord Admiral of the Ocean Sea.' "

MUSIC AND GEOGRAPHY

Romano never showed any great personal interest in music. But the world of music was interested in him. Dr. Wanderman recalls how Romano once stuck needles through the hypnotized Mrs. Josef Hofmann's cheeks. Romano had the center of the stage on this memorable occasion. Present at the meeting were Rachmaninoff and his gifted uncle, Saladi, also Glazunov, Rosenthal, Bruno Walther, "Popsy" Godowsky, Josef Hofmann, and George Gershwin.

Romano once said:

"Russia has vast, cold, flat steppes. Russia's music is dark and melancholy. It sounds as though they are afraid of freezing to death. Germany and Austria have high, snow-capped mountains, and the people live in deep valleys. In order to get out of their mountain surroundings, they needed heroes, which were symbolized by various brass instruments: horns and drums. Italy has a mellow climate and varied terrain. Its music is melodious, with gay, long tones. The Negroes in Africa are half-naked in their hot jungles. They are not self-conscious and nothing seems to inhibit them. They developed erotic, lively music: jazz."

* * *

Although his timing and details were off, in the darkest days of World War II, Romano foresaw only defeat for Hitler's Third Reich. Bidding goodbye to a reporter, Carl W. McCardle of the Philadelphia *Evening Bulletin,* March 2, 1942, he said, "Hitler will commit suicide before this year is over." The New York *World Telegram,* in Romano's obituary, recalled his prediction: ". . . nearly three years before the event that, 'Hitler will commit suicide as soon as he has some bad reverses. He'll shoot himself; he wouldn't have the heart to cut himself or jump out a window.' "

GOOSESTEPPING

"Goosestepping made slaves out of the Germans. They clicked their heels and responded to commands of life or death. They suffered from mob psychology. They responded quickly to hate, because hating others gave them a feeling of superiority. When you goosestep you must so keep your mind on balance that you cannot think, and you annihilate all individual reasoning powers."

PRINCESS HOHENLOHE

In his book about espionage in World War II, *Room 3603* (Farrar, Straus & Co., New York, 1963), Montgomery Hyde described a "clever, scheming Austrian who bore some resemblance to the glamorous spy of fiction." Her Serene Highness Princess Stephanie Hohenlohe-Waldenberg-Schillingsfurst had a generously inscribed photograph from Adolf Hitler and was cited in the House of Commons as a "notorious member of the Hitler spy organization." Here is Jacques Romano's description of his encounter with this dangerous woman.

"Princess Stephanie Hohenlohe was a German princess working for Hitler. In 1938 she came to New York to see me, having heard about me in England. She was staying in New York at the Waldorf-Astoria, and had the largest suite on the 42nd floor. It was March 16, 1938, the day before St. Patrick's day. I made an appointment to meet her at 5:00 P.M. and arrived a few minutes early. She had already instructed the elevator operator to bring me up to see her. She said she would be five minutes late. This was to impress me with her royalty. I decided to wait. Finally I went up. We met. She kissed me on the cheek, and I kissed her on the cheek and then her hand. She said, 'Now, Mr. Romano, I have heard so much about you, and I have confidence in you.'

"After exchanging pleasantries for a few moments, she asked me if I knew a particular man in New York whom she had come to hate. She said she had met him in England and that because she trusted me she was telling me how she wanted to see this man killed. I said, 'Well, you'll get over it.'

"By her conversation I immediately recognized this as an old secret service trick. She would know that if her information about wanting to kill the man got out, the story could have originated only from me and that I, therefore, could not keep my mouth shut. Her confidence and requests for a favor were really ways of testing me.

"She then asked me, 'Are you ready to go to Europe with me on the *Queen Mary* next week? Mr. Romano, you are a great psychic and Hitler is a psychic, and the two of you could do great things for humanity!' I told her, 'My dear Princess, I have never claimed to be a psychic, but I am interested in psychic phenomena. Furthermore, I have made a study of Hitler and have concluded that he is not psychic but psychopathic.' That ended my prospects of meeting Hitler. However, the princess kept her composure and then, perhaps, betrayed her own doubts of Hitler's psychic abilities, as well as her own attitude toward him, by asking me countless questions about her future and about her son who was working for Henry Ford in Detroit. I left."

VIII

HELPING A HEALTHY BODY
STAY YOUNG

"I have perfect control over my body."

ALTHOUGH he never had a formal education, Romano lectured to doctors and dentists on suggestive therapeutics and geriatrics. He discovered a series of organic iodine medicines. He was a founding and the only lay member of the exclusive physicians' club, The Medical Strollers (New York), and an honorary Doctor of Osteopathy of the Philadelphia College and the Infirmary of Osteopathy. He was hypnotist for Dr. Henry W. Frauenthal's clinic of the Hospital for Deformities and Joint Diseases (New York).

It is interesting that Jacques Romano, who was known to many people as a healer, was seldom, if ever, seen to have a head cold. He had a lifelong romance with the subject of health for body and mind.

Let us, then, listen to Romano, the man of flesh and blood, and study his body machinery, some of his astonishing Yogi-like stunts, and his handwriting. What sort of man is it that throughout most of his ninety-eight years was mistaken for someone considerably younger, or even on occasion, for his own father?

BEING YOUR OWN GRANDPA

"In 1940, an acquaintance asked me to speak at the Real Estate Appraisers' Banquet. He said I could tell them many interesting things from my years of living in New York and that they would be particularly interested in my reminiscences of Steve Brody, Lillian Russell, De Wolf Hopper, Al Smith, and others. After the lecture, during which I included some of my experiences in the Orient, a decrepit old man came up to me and said, 'I enjoyed your talk on ancient philosophy very much. I once heard a man speak of this many, many years ago. He must certainly be dead by this time, because he was of your age in those days. I wonder, though, if he might have been your father.' I turned around and said, 'Did you hear him speak on Henry Street, at the office of Dr. Lesser?' He said, 'Why, yes!' I said, 'I am the same old man!'"

From his earliest manhood Romano used to step up to the lectern, point his finger at his audience, and boldly proclaim that he was going to live one hundred and fifty years! Although Romano had no birth certificate, it was possible by circumstantial evidence to establish his claimed age as a reasonable assumption. His comments, autographed photographs, correspondence, and reported adventures agreed with his stated age. Other sources tending to confirm his age included an elderly friend, Carl Stehle of New York, a former associate of John Hays Hammond. Mr. Stehle wrote that he remembered Romano was then fifty years of age.

Evidence authenticating his age comes from Mrs. Bessie Mitchell Boehm of New York, who with her family knew Romano when she was a young girl in Shrewsbury, New

Jersey, and from a distinguished jurist, Judge John Warren Hill of New York, who remembered Romano when he was a boy. Dr. Abraham J. Ginsberg, the eminent ear, nose, and throat specialist and inventor of medical electronic apparatus, also knew Romano from near the turn of the century and tended to confirm his age as claimed. (See Chapter 10 for their reminiscences.)

Dr. Seymour S. Wanderman, Romano's personal physician, wrote that he knew Romano more than forty years and, although he had no positive proof, he believed his true age as claimed. Romano's age was always consistent for the forty years, and his wife Molly believed that Jacques was as old as he said he was. Furthermore, Dr. Wanderman met physicians and other people who had known his very unusual patient in the past, and through complex circumstances it always seemed that Romano's claimed age agreed with their knowledge.

E. Swift Newton of Croydon Hutch, Anselma, Pennsylvania, asserted that Romano was born the same year as his father, A. Edward Newton. The elder Newton was the noted essayist and bibliophile and "one of the most colorful literary figures of the century." From their many discussions, A. E. Newton was satisfied that Romano was the age he claimed to be. Also, various newspaper accounts since 1929, and such friends as Dr. Frederick C. Heyer of New York, gave ages which tended to coincide with his claimed age.

Romano, as was earlier described, had charge of the Eastman Kodak Company exhibit at the Buffalo Exposition in 1901. It is hardly likely that a boy would have held such a responsible position. One of the best evidences for Romano's age was obtained from his early employer in the United States, the Eastman Kodak Company:

May 18, 1956

Dear Dr. Schwarz:

In your letter of May 10th you requested certain information about one of our former employees, Mr. Jacques Romano, in connection with certain psychiatric research which you are conducting.

Unfortunately, our personal records prior to 1920 are not especially complete. Because of this we are unable to give you exact information regarding his dates of employment with us nor his age. However, the following information was uncovered in our investigation of the problem which may be of interest to you.

Mr. Armin Baltzer, the present Manager of our sales operations in the South American countries, remembers Mr. Romano as having been a representative for us in that area in 1914 when Mr. Baltzer joined that department. It is his recollection that Mr. Romano worked for us approximately from 1907 to approximately 1915.

To verify his thinking, Mr. Baltzer communicated with Mr. José Aponte who is one of our retirees from that department. Mr. Aponte, who is presently seventy-five years of age, stated that Mr. Romano was about fifteen years older than he at the time they worked together in the Export Sales Department. Mr. Aponte made this statement without having seen your letter and without knowing that Mr. Romano claims to be ninety-two years old.

I hope that this information will be of some help to you. I regret that we are able to provide you only with statements of opinion and not with absolute facts based on specific records. If we can be of further help to you, we are more than happy to try.

Yours very truly,
(signed) N. W. Spies
Personnel Director
Kodak Office

For these many reasons, then, Romano's age would appear to be as he stated it.

*   *   *

In his middle nineties Romano was an unusual physical specimen. The cold statistics are: 5'5¼" tall; 115 pounds; blood pressure 130/72; wiry, athletic frame; clear unblemished and unwrinkled skin; a full head of greying to black hair; twinkling eyes; crisp, succinct manner of speech, and indefinably accented English; a firm, low tenor voice—but all these are not as descriptive as a photograph.

In technical jargon, Romano's physical deficits were minimal. They were limited to a nonincapacitating, moderate, pill-rolling tremor (Parkinsonian) of the right hand, and moderate enlargement of the prostate gland. Of more significance is the fact that until almost the very end of his life he appeared and acted like a man twenty to thirty years younger. The palpation of his arteries in the extremities revealed him to be relatively youthful. An eye specialist, who was associated with a New York medical school, reported the appearance of the vessels deep within the eyeballs suggested the condition of a man more than twenty-five years younger than his stated age. When Romano first noticed some hearing difficulty at age ninety-six, he was examined by Dr. Hector R. Giancarlo, Director of Research, New York Eye and Ear Infirmary, who reported: "Taking into account the patient's age, this is considered a minimal loss."

Elaborate studies by a specialist in internal medicine, Dr. George P. Balz of the University of Cincinnati Medical School (Ohio), established that Romano was healthy in all his organs and free of the stigmata of disease. X rays of the head, hands, chest, and legs were within normal limits. There was no significant evidence of hardening of the arteries or of arthritic changes. Electrocardiograms and electroencephalograms (brain waves) similarly revealed no evidence of malfunction.

Careful laboratory analyses of Romano's blood and urine revealed no evidence of disease or disturbance of function. His fasting blood sugar, serum cholesterol, and esters and blood urea nitrogen determinations were all well within normal limits. His basic metabolic rate (B.M.R.) had to be calculated like that of a younger person, since the graphs did not extend to anywhere near his age group. However, compared with the oldest standardized age (79), Romano's B.M.R. was plus 1, or completely consistent with health, and suggestive of how efficiently his body thermostat controlled the combustion of energy.

YOGI-LIKE FEATS

For many years Romano amazed people by his ability to stop his radial pulses, race and slow his pulses in both upper extremities, and make one hand blanch white while the other became swollen and red. He did indeed do these things, but obviously not by stopping his heart. Romano accelerated or slowed his pulse indirectly by thinking of emotional states associated with a fast or slow rate. He would quietly think of frightening situations or pleasant relaxing conditions. Careful electrocardiographic (ECG) studies failed to reveal, however, any consistently quantitative changes in his heart rate when he attempted to race, slow, or stop his pulse. The particular wave forms and units of time recorded also showed no consistent changes. He probably stopped his pulse by contracting some of the muscles that surround the subclavian and axillary arteries, which are embedded in the chest, the neck, and under the armpit regions. This, however, is quite a feat for anyone to perform. Try it! Perhaps, in a similar fashion, he could cause one hand to blanch while the other became swollen and red.

Another of Romano's Yogi-like abilities was the capac-

ity to fall into a deep sleep almost at will. The electro-
encephalographic (brain wave) studies completely confirmed this because, while sitting in an ordinary, straight-
backed office chair, during a brain wave test, Romano
closed his eyes and within 230 seconds was in a deep, ob-
jectively verified, physiological sleep. This is a most unusual ability. Although some people assert they can do
this, most of them usually go into a trancelike state, not
unlike a hypnotic catalepsy, or a state of sleepwalking. In
any event, this kind of "sleep," although possibly related
to true physiological sleep, is quite different from Romano's feat, and can be readily distinguished by the particular brain wave patterns. It can be conjectured that the
ability to go into a deep, true sleep at will is one reason
that Romano had such phenomenal energy and apparently
did well with a minimal amount of sleep during the night.
He was able to take frequent periods of refreshing sleep
during the day. He could entrance himself and thus shut
out all exhausting, and often destructive, sources of extraneous stimulation. He learned to respond selectively to
matters of consequence. He thus evidenced amazing control over his body.

HANDWRITING

When studied by an expert, a man's handwriting can
frequently give clues about his state of health and personality. Different diseases and emotional states can often
first be detected in a handwriting specimen. As has been
noted, in addition to his widespread psychic and artistic
talents, Romano had experiences where he, himself, was

a handwriting expert. For this reason it seemed fair to turn the tables and seek the opinion of a handwriting expert on Romano's writing. A letter was penned by Romano and submitted to Kenneth W. Thompson, M.D., who, in addition to his duties as Medical Director and Research Vice-President of Organon, Inc.,* is widely recognized for his ability as a handwriting expert. This is one of Dr. Thompson's hobbies, and on many television shows and elsewhere he has often made amazingly correct deductions and interpretations. When he received the Romano letter, Dr. Thompson knew nothing about Romano, but entered into the spirit of the study and made the following nontechnical interpretive analysis.

"There is a small amount of tremor but remarkably little for what appears to be an old person. The pressure suggests lots of vitality and vigor. There is a disturbed variation in the form and adjustment. The size of the letters is inconsistent. English is not his native language. The 'Jacques' is very naturally written with Latin curves, but the 'Romano' is not. That could be something different. In other respects the writing is of a romance language type.

"There are impractical, unreal bursts; the wandering from a line might mean that the path of action in everyday life is not steady, that the subject has lost some of his control and ability to give careful attention to details. The writing also suggests a 'take it or leave it attitude' or 'this is it.' There is a sweep or emphasis on declamation, a fluctuation of pressure and punctuated speech. This is

* Dr. Thompson is currently Research Professor of Obstetrics and Gynecology at the University of Wisconsin Medical School. A recent article of his, "Graphology and the Physician," appeared in the *Journal of the American Medical Association*, Vol. 194, No. 3, October 19, 1965, p. 312.

consistent with blowing off of steam and possibly lots of aggression. The strong down strokes suggest that his instinctual life has been diverted. Although it would appear that he (still) has much instinctual life and many sexual requirements, there is also indication of an extreme variability in his physical drive, which at other times might be quite feeble. He has been so involved with the sexual and physical requirements that his life was in danger of being disturbed by these. But he learned how to interpose will power and control them. There is much fantasy connected with his instinctual and sexual life. In this way he releases tension below the level of reality.

"He sees things as black or white, right or wrong and with little modulation in between. Furthermore, he knows when he is right. He is more the mathematician and engineer in contrast to the ordinary Latin who sees things in compromises. He has a good sense of structure as in architecture and sculpture. He is not particularly poetic, rhythmical, or musical. This man is almost Germanic in his abrupt motions. He does not go out of his way to make interpersonal relationships, and is not easygoing. He is normally possessive, critical, opinionated, meticulous, and perseverative in doing little things. He feels cramped mentally and possibly has lost faith in himself; yet he does not feel dependent and prostrate. He uses discrimination in bulling through obstacles. He has little fear and is practical in his approach.

"He is emotionally balanced and has an adjusted state of euphoria. He is trying to control this and the minor fluctuations with depression. He feels, 'Jacques is a good fellow,' and he wants the world to think well of him. For this he requires little or no significant capital outlay, material things or elegant surroundings. He dwells on the past in relation to his physical self. Something has happened to him in the past, a serious injury or threat to life. He has a good sense of social organization and considerable competence in getting a message across. The letters 'J R' in his signature suggest a once vigorous man, yet the small 'q' is suggestive of the influence of old age. His name is in the center and he must be in the center of the stage. He does not require ego recognition, and, in everyday life, is modest. He is not hampered by people around him and he feels recognition in himself. He does not deceive himself and is completely honest. He is not an outgoing personality to the world. All endings are unpleasant. He does not pay attention to how he makes or breaks with people. He is not a typically religious man, yet he is drawing crosses everywhere. He sees life as a mutual process or scheme and he has his own exact way of meeting obstacles. His writing is similar to that of people between sixty-five and seventy years of age."

IX

ROMANO'S "RAY"

"I felt an ice-cold wind emanating from his finger."
—*Sunday Chronicle,* FEBRUARY 2, 1936

ROMANO'S "ray" was perceived as a cool-breezelike sensation. Romano, who was ninety-five years of age when this study was undertaken, claimed he had had his "ray" since early childhood. Many newspaper articles about him throughout the years mentioned this strange ability. He recalled: "I could do something that others could not. At twelve I discovered how I could hold my outstretched hands over children and quiet them. I could even stop a baby's crying. Later, I found I could relieve headaches in the same manner. As a young man, I met a wise man who gave me an explanation for this strange ability. He said that we all radiated from our bodies, and he illustrated this by holding a handkerchief in his hand for a few seconds and then giving it to me. It seemed as if there was a very slight, cool breeze coming from the handkerchief. I learned that the human body is surrounded by a mysterious envelope or radiation, a strong force that I have no name for. Many people have commented on this through the years.

"My wife Molly, and our neighbors in the country, were often amazed to see how the plants and flowers I 'radiated' frequently grew many times larger than the other flowers I did not treat. The only person who seriously studied this phenomenon and who was interested in my 'ray' was Professor Otto Rahn of Cornell University."

Romano's "ray"* might best be defined by describing it in action. For instance, Romano would ask a subject to hold out his hand. He then brought the tip of one finger close to the subject's hand, and the subject experienced tingling in the hand. When Romano was successful, as he usually was, the subject was startled and amused by the resulting tingling effects. The "ray" could "go through" a telephone book, a glass ashtray, an earthenware flower pot, and thin sheets of (copper, brass, aluminum, iron, and lead) objects. When these objects were placed between Romano's fingers and the subject's outstretched hand, the results were always the same. The effects could also be transmitted to the subject's hand from Romano's outstretched foot through his leather shoes and cotton socks. While he was "radiating," there was no striking change in Romano's pulse, respiratory rate, or general appearance. His two hands appeared similar on gross inspection when he was "radiating."

The "ray" produced similar results in men and women of all ages. Many who willingly participated in these studies were physicians and scientists of varying disciplines. Their incredulous attitude and professed resistance to "suggestion" did not affect their ability to perceive correctly. Sometimes they reported that the "ray" was perceived faintly or not at all. At other times there was a

* For supportive tables and graphs, see *Parapsychology*, Vol. 5, No. 3, 1963–64, pp. 113–127.

strong tingling, cool-breezelike sensation. Romano himself was often unaware of the strength of his "ray." Even when the subject was blindfolded and had cotton in his ears, he immediately and correctly localized the cool sensation to various parts of his body, his right or left hand, forehead, cheek, chin, nose, ear, and so forth. When an unsuspecting three-year-old girl was blindfolded and merely instructed to "sit still for a little game" (in a room that was 70° F.), she said, "It's cold in the kitchen, it's cold!" every time Romano applied his "ray" to parts of her face or hands.

On many occasions the "ray" transiently bent a candle flame, even when the candle was shielded with a glass chimney. This effect was more apparent and pronounced than when other people, presumably without such an emanation, tried to do the same thing. However, this simple test with the candle flame was vitiated because in the process of "radiating" Romano raised his hand to the area he was attempting to affect. Thus, it was difficult to separate the possible breeze caused by Romano's movement from the cooling sensation due to the "ray." When an ordinary alcohol thermometer was used as a target for the "ray," there were no temperature changes. On other occasions, there was no discernible effect on an electroscope even though the subjective cooling effects were perceived.

Because of Romano's apparent extraordinary psychic abilities and his presumed telepathic suggestion with playing cards, it was felt that he might have produced the cooling effects of his "ray" in an analogous manner. That is, he could subtly induce a telepathic skin hallucination which the subjects then correctly localized and interpreted as a cool breeze. One way of attempting to get around this experimental defect was to have Romano "radiate" films that are used in clinical X-ray work. On numerous trials no clearcut effects could be discerned. Similarly, when numerous infra-red photographs were taken of Romano, when he was in a trancelike state, nothing out of the ordinary was observed. Also when the "ray" was tested by Dr. Sigurd E. Johnsen in a scintillation apparatus, for possible radioactivity, there was no effect.

Another way of studying the "ray" was provided by Romano's mention of once meeting the late Professor Otto Rahn* of Cornell. That scientist, after many years of study, concluded that some human beings have radiations that can affect the growth of yeast cultures. Accordingly, in this investigation, some experiments were undertaken in which Romano "radiated" test tubes of presumed equal amounts of yeast cells growing in various concentrations of sugar solutions. However, because of the difficulties in accurately controlling these studies, this method was abandoned in favor of a simpler technique. From correspondence with Dr. J. B. Rhine, the author heard about plant growth experiments and prayer; and from another source it was concluded that "prayer can make a difference in the speed of seed germination and the rate and vigor of plant growth." Thus, Romano's "ray" was tried on the germination and growth of ordinary sunflower seeds and hybrid corn.

These experiments were undertaken in Romano's ninety-fifth year, when he possessed good general health and appeared to have his "ray." His only outstanding different dietary or drug habit was that he regularly took his own proprietary iodine preparation, Liquidine. For forty years he had taken fifteen drops of this twice a day.

* Rahn, Otto, *Invisible Radiations of Organisms,* Verlag von Gebruder Borntraeger, Vol. 9, 1936, 215 pp.

On eleven different occasions, when he "felt like it,"
Romano, for periods varying from one to seven minutes,
at various intervals usually consisting of several seconds,
"radiated" one hundred or more sunflower seeds* or hybrid corn seeds* that had been planted in a commercially
prepared soil. While he "radiated" these seeds, another
batch of seeds, similarly prepared and placed in identical
companion aluminum or plastic (methylstyrene) trays, was
exposed to the same room temperature and prevailing
conditions. It was possible to subjectively test Romano's
"ray" before he actually "radiated" the seeds. When the
"radiation" was completed, the lids were put back on all
the containers and they were then placed together on a
shelf for three to five days. After that time the trays were
opened and the number of seeds that had germinated was
counted and the growth of the roots and stems was carefully measured in millimeters. As an additional precaution, a double-blind technique was used on two occasions
when Dr. B. A. Ruggieri or the author's wife witnessed
and timed Romano's "radiations." No one but Dr. Ruggieri knew which seeds were "treated" and which were
not, until a third party, Mrs. Isabelle M. Sayre, the author's secretary, had completely measured and calculated,
with an adding machine, all the indices of germination
and growth. In all the experiments Mrs. Sayre had no
knowledge of which seeds were treated and which were
untreated controls until she finished her calculations and
was given the correct key.

As a final method of attempting to control these studies,
the author, who has no "ray," stimulated in eleven experi-

* Seeds of known genetic background made available through the
kindness of W. Atlee Burpee Company, Seed Growers, Philadelphia,
Pennsylvania.

ments the "radiation" of batches of seeds under conditions analogous to those used with Romano. In the instance of both Romano and the author they subjectively felt that they were stimulating all the seeds they "radiated" for increased germination and growth.

The data were then statistically scrutinized by Miss Elizabeth L. Babcock, who prepared illustrative tables and graphs. Although Miss Babcock felt that a greater number of samples would have been statistically desirable, she consented to review the data after being told of some of the technical difficulties.

* * *

The overall figures revealed some interesting results. Of 1,400 sunflower seeds Romano "radiated," 410 germinated, whereas in his control of 1,400 seeds that were not "radiated," 427 germinated. The suppressive effect of radiation, 4.0 per cent, was not a statistically significant difference. However, in the author's "mock radiation" of 1,100 sunflower seeds, 339 germinated, or an insignificant difference of 0.6 per cent. Thus, it was concluded that the control (mock) "ray" did not affect germination of sunflower seeds.

When hybrid corn seeds were used, there was no effect on germination either for Romano and his "ray" or the author and his (mock) "ray." Out of 850 seeds "radiated" by Romano, 386 germinated, whereas out of 850 "nonradiated" seeds, 283 germinated, for a germination-stimulating effect of 0.8 per cent. The author, using 1,000 hybrid corn seeds, obtained 481 germinated, by simulated radiation, and 485 for the nontreated group of 1,000 seeds. The difference was a paltry 0.8 per cent. Thus, it was concluded that for both Romano's "ray" and the simulated controls by the author there was no startling difference or suggestion of any effect on germination while using hybrid corn seeds.

However, there were some measurable growth effects. By measuring in millimeters the total stems and roots of Romano's "radiated" and "nonradiated" sunflower seeds and comparing them with seeds treated in a simulated fashion by the author, some differences were apparent. In seven experiments using 1,400 sunflower seeds for "radiation" and 1,400 as a control, Romano exerted a highly significant percentage of growth suppression effect of 19.1 per cent (total growth suppression, 26.9 per cent). The author, with simulated "radiated" and untreated batches of 1,100 sunflower seeds in six experiments, obtained an insignificant difference of −5.7 per cent (total growth suppression, −1.7 per cent).

In the instance of growth of hybrid corn, though, there were no significant growth effects. Using 850 seeds of corn which he "radiated" and an untreated control of 850 seeds, Romano produced a growth-stimulating effect of −0.1 per cent (−1.8 per cent, total growth suppression). The author, using 1,000 seeds each for the simulated "radiated" and untreated batches, produced a growth-suppressive effect of 2.5 per cent (0.2 per cent, total growth suppression).

For all experiments, it was impossible to correlate any presumed seed effects with the subjectively perceived strength of Romano's "ray."

*   *   *

It is a curious fact that under the described experimental conditions Romano's emanation apparently suppressed the growth of sunflower seeds and yet did not affect their germination or the germination and growth of hybrid corn. In a comparable series of experiments, the author obtained no significant differences between those sunflower seeds and corn that were and those that were not treated with his (mock) "ray." Thus, except for the two variables of Romano's "ray" and the author's (mock) "ray," essentially similar conditions prevailed throughout all the seed experiments. Although more experiments would have been statistically desirable, it is reasonable to assume that the particular methodology and controls make chance, and factors like humidity, light, and electrical disturbances, unlikely explanations for the suppressive growth effect of Romano's "ray" on sunflower seeds.

The apparent suppressive effect of Romano's "ray" on sunflower-seed growth showed no correlation with the subjectively perceived strength of his "ray" or his declared intention of "stimulating growth." Why a "ray" that a person can apparently perceive through lead and various other materials should affect sunflower-seed growth and not influence hybrid corn is the question. Possibly this strange effect is related to the different structure and function of the sunflower and hybrid corn seeds. It should be noted that Professor Rahn quoted many experiments where different indicators, like onion root tip, yeasts, and so forth, showed widely varying sensitivities to mitogenetic radiations.

If these preliminary experiments suggest the objective existence of Romano's "ray," then, in addition to studying the seeds that were affected, there is the equally important problem of understanding the physiological mechanisms related to the "ray." Thus, the problem of experimental technique is vastly complicated in such a study because it must fit the conditions of Romano rather than vice versa. Therefore, any possible experimental variations, such as using different time intervals, species of seeds, and so forth, must be secondary to the phenomenon under study —a human "ray." More experiments would have to be undertaken to verify the results. However, because of the rather complicated human factors that seemed to be a prerequisite for Romano's "ray," this was all that was obtained.

What clues might there be for a relationship between Romano's "ray" and his emotional attitude? The Reverend F. Loehr, in his book *The Power of Prayer on Plants*, reported rather marked effects on both the speed of germination and rate and vigor of plant growth that he attributed to the "power of prayer." It might follow that if prayer can produce such effects, and for the purpose of this study its definition might include a person's conscious and unconscious attitude with any concomitant psychosomatic changes (telekinesis? radiations?), then such factors as these would also have to be considered in the Romano experiments. This intriguing possibility of the influence of attitudes was limited, for the most part, to Romano by use of a double-blind technique where the attitude of the persons connected with the experiments (the author's wife, Dr. Ruggieri, and the author) other than Romano could not have easily "influenced" the growth of the particular seeds that Romano "radiated."

In contrast to Romano's "ray," it should be emphasized that in the author's experiments with his (mock) "ray" there was no effect other than chance. Now, the author's emotional status was quite different from Romano's and, unlike Romano, he has no striking telepathic-clairvoyant abilities. For these reasons, then (Romano's intrinsic control and control with the author), the rate-of-sunflower-seed-growth results support the subjective human experience that Romano had an emanation and that the paresthetic effects he produced in human beings were not solely subjective, telepathic, or due to suggestion. The intriguing question still unanswered is: Was Romano's "ray" related to his emotional attitude and, if so, in what way?

Another outstanding difference between Romano and most other people was his history of the daily ingestion of an iodine-containing solution, Liquidine, for more than forty years. It might be wondered if this, of itself, could in some way account for a radiating effect. Certainly patients who take iodine-containing drugs (e.g., Lugol's Solution) in lesser or comparable dosages than Romano took Liquidine have never been observed to develop side effects analogous to a "ray": i.e., ability to produce cool-breeze emanations from the hands or feet. For this reason, as well as the fact that long before Romano started taking iodine some of his friends were aware of the subjective effects of his "ray," it is unlikely that the iodine contributed to production of the "ray."

In addition to Loehr's studies, some indirect support for the viewpoint that Romano's "ray" was related to his attitude and telepathic-clairvoyant abilities may be derived from several other sources. For example, in accounts of the famous medium, D. D. Home, "cold air blowing around" was noted before various telekinetic phenomena occurred. Similarly, the noted psychic researcher, Hereward Carrington, and others noticed a cool breeze issuing from the forehead and finger of the medium Eusapia Palladino during her seances. There are also reports of cold air being perceived in the presence of the entranced clergyman medium, Stainton Moses. Also, the parapsychologist

Tyrell has collected several cases where the sensation of cold was associated with the perception of an apparition. Cool-breeze effects have also been reported as concomitants to possible telepathic death perceptions.

Such reports as these suggest that, if one's attitude or the possession of psychic abilities might be a prerequisite for the occurrence of such phenomena as a cool-breeze effect, then this relationship might be one explanation for the reported conflicting effects of so-called mitogenetic radiations.*

In his scholarly monograph, Professor Rahn often quoted the work of others as well as his own experiences. Gurwitsch, the Russian scientist, told Rahn: "All investigators using biological detectors have had the experience of sudden failures of cultures to react, and such a condition usually remained for several days or even for a number of weeks and it was impossible to produce even the simplest mitogenetic effect. Eventually the culture reacted normally again. The author, himself, has had long periods of negative results in his laboratory and they come and go at irregular intervals. If the cause should prove to be of such general nature as, e.g., weather, cosmic rays, terrestrial magnetism, or sunspots, it might be that the senders do not function under the prevailing conditions: greatly intensified susceptibility of living detectors by rhythmic discontinuity of radiations."†

Perhaps the subtle emotional attitudes (psychophysiological effects?) of the different investigators have been a hitherto ignored factor in these particular investigations. Although such a hypothesis of attitude affecting mito-

---

* Glasser, O., Medical Physics, Vol. I, *Mitogenetic Radiation*, Chicago, The Year Book Publishers, 1947, pp. 760–763.
† Rahn, *op. cit.*

genesis or growth might be highly speculative, it is not inconsistent with some of the disparate results obtained by different investigators and by the same investigator at varying times. It would be in keeping with such a hypothesis to anticipate such apparently contradictory data. Such an experience of having an effect one time and not another would not be unlike the clinical observation that telepathy often occurs in clusters for a period of time, then submerges from awareness only to return in force at a much later time.

Rahn* noted how some menstruating women had a "harmful emanation" that could produce changes in yeasts and bacteria. He speculated about a "menotoxin" which he related to oxycholesterol, and he wondered if this "menotoxin" could account for such practical commercial problems as the wilting of flowers used for French perfume factories, ruining mushroom beds, making bread dough that would not rise normally, and packing pickles and sauerkraut that would not keep. He also quoted documented instances of adverse effects of such an emanation in the dairy industry, where poor cultures were obtained, and in the making of improperly fermented wine.

Attention might also be directed to some recent and well-controlled laboratory studies by Grad,† of McGill University. By the use of ingenious techniques, the effectiveness of a healer was brilliantly demonstrated. He could influence wound healing in mice and also could produce a presumed telekinetic effect on plant growth.

* *Ibid.*

† Grad, B., Cadoret, R. J., and Paul, G. I., An Unorthodox Method of Treatment on Wound Healing in Mice, *International Journal of Parapsychology*, Vol. III, No. 2, 1961, pp. 5–24. Grad, B., A Telekinetic Effect on Plant Growth, *International Journal of Parapsychology*, Vol. V, No. 2, 1963, pp. 113–117.

Another source of evidence about possible human emanation but from a different discipline is provided by Father Thurston, the distinguished scholar and hagiographer, who reported phenomena similar to the "ray" in the lives of various saints. He particularly cited studies by Protti on the "luminous woman" of Pirano. Thurston's reference was a report from the *Times* and it stated that the radiant power of the woman's blood was three times normal during her religious fast. Unfortunately, as Thurston maintained, no other information was given. However, Rahn mentioned several studies on human radiation (with different subjects) by the same investigator, Protti.

In addition to Rahn's account of mitogenetic radiation, recent work by Borthwick and Hendricks has shown varying growth responses of different seeds that were exposed, for a relatively short length of time, to different applications of radiant energy. Thus, if Romano's induced tingling was not in part or whole a suggestively and/or telepathically induced hallucination, then an emanation that can be subjectively perceived to "pass through" an element of such high atomic weight as lead could be hypothesized to be of apparent short-wave length and of high energy. Although the human subjective data and the objective sunflower growth effects are two different things, it is difficult to see how an emanation that can apparently pass through lead has such a minimal biological effect.

Before leaving the baffling subject of Romano's "ray," mention might be made of his theory about the extinction of prehistoric monsters.

"Professor Millikan (noted physicist) asked me what reason I could offer for the existence, and subsequent extinction, of prehistoric monsters. I said that one reason for the dinosaurs, lizards, mastodons, and giant birds which existed millions of years ago was that, at that early period, in evolution, the moon was still alive and an independent planet. Perhaps the moon gave off rays that stimulated growth on earth. When the moon died, the rays ceased, and the giant beasts died out."

X

HOW ROMANO
CONTROLLED HIS PSYCHIC ABILITIES

*"Telepathy is based on a hunch or feeling. It is a bond
between two people."*

THE first telepathic incident Romano could recall was
when he was about six years old.* His father, in the
course of seeking medical help, had gone to a special clinic
near Königsberg, Germany. While there, he stayed at a
particular hotel. Upon returning home, he and Jacques's
mother were discussing the trip, which was a therapeutic
failure, and they tried to remember the name of the hotel.
Jacques, with no previous knowledge of the name of the
place, blurted out that it was the "Pomerantz Hotel,"
which was correct. His parents looked at each other in
astonishment and wondered what was the matter with
their son. Jacques also recalled how he had correctly in-
formed his parents of all the visitors they had had when
they were away from home on the trip to Germany.

"The first glance is all I needed to remember the people
who came to visit my parents while they were away. When

---

* As far as he was aware, no one else in his family had presumed
telepathic abilities. Jacques Romano had telepathy until the day before
his death at ninety-eight and a half years of age.

they returned, weeks later, I drew pictures so my parents could tell who they were."

In these early years Jacques thought of "devils, ghosts, and spirits walking at me. I used to dream of the Orient. I wanted to see spirits. One night when I was about seven, I awakened in my room and thought I saw a tall Oriental man with a turban. I watched him hold his chin in his hand. He came closer and closer and then disappeared under the bed. I carefully crawled under the bed and looked for him, without awakening my brother, but there was nothing to be seen. It was a phantom vision. Because of my desire I had had a wish-fulfillment hallucination. The dream was so vivid that it persisted for a short while even though my eyes were open and I became wider awake."

Throughout the travels of his early manhood Jacques gradually developed a "cold-blooded ability to observe the strength and weaknesses of human beings and an ability to sense danger." He learned the art of minimizing his own personality and making himself subject to the moods and feelings of those with whom he came in contact. Thus, he discovered that he often could recite events that had occurred in a person's life.

"When I sit near someone, I begin to 'feel' his knowledge. I am susceptible to his thoughts and vibrations. It is as if I had heard them before and I was trying to recall them. The sounds and words are tangible things that occurred. I do not do 'mind reading,' but I tell people about things that happened to them in their past. I feel the influence of their experiences which I interpret in my own language, things that they, themselves, frequently have difficulty in remembering. A thought is an action. Any thought that ever was set forth from the time of the

Egyptians until today still vibrates, and the identity is still there. The philosophers merely repeat what was said five to six thousand years ago. There is nothing new.

"If I am near physicians, I am sensitive to the influence of their knowledge. For instance, although I do not know anatomy, I can feel the different types of pain associated with various diseases. I have surprised physicians by mimicking past, personal illnesses with the salient clinical features. I've had similar experiences from contacts with artists, philosophers, and scientists. When I 'read a person's mind' I feel very sympathetic toward that person. I have put myself completely in his shoes.

"Telepathy is based on a hunch or feeling. It is a bond between two people. Like a game, telepathy must be friendly and you must like to do it. I must be literally and figuratively warm and I become enthusiastic. If, while I am doing this telepathic work, there is any criticism or combativeness, I lose my passivity and no longer care. I am very sensitive to anyone's 'wrong' opinion. As long as it [the telepathic 'mind reading'] does not mean anything and there is no resistance [combativeness, anxiety], it just comes to me. I ask myself and wonder what it means. I just attune myself to one condition. It is like a musical ear. Aggressiveness or an attempt to use this ability commercially only seems to undermine the necessary passivity for the development of the state and the production of phenomena. If I force myself with this talent, I am no good at all. If I am wrong, I bite my lip, stop, and then start all over again. In doing this, I never condemn the other person. It is I who is wrong. I have to be able to control it.

"Presentiments and hunches are beams between two people who like each other and think of each other. I can sometimes feel the bombardment from another person who is interested in the same work as I am. As an example, I remember the Patent Office asking me about two inventors, one in New York and the other in San Francisco. They had identical inventions and had come into the Patent Office within one hour of each other. It was not a new phenomenon to me. They must have both received the same vibrations.

"Not infrequently I have had presentiment of when someone I knew, or had just met, would die. In arriving at this I put myself up as a standard of perfect health and life everlasting. Then, as I think of the person in question I compare him with my health and life, his horsepower with my horsepower. Maybe he does not look as though he would live five months or maybe five years in comparison with me. By educating myself to be receptive to truth and reality, to accept the facts whatever they are, I have often been able to perceive vibrations and correctly foretell a death. However, I am careful about this because, in addition to errors, there is the risk of implanting a very destructive suggestion.

"When perceiving vibrations, I am not interested in anybody's affairs, gossip, or opinions. When I read a mind I never look at the person. I must be sensitive to conditions (facts, realities). Interest is such a motive of inquisitiveness that it leads to a constant social turmoil (anxiety) in my mind. Therefore, without any motive for compliments or praise, I am open to suggestions (telepathy), and the things I say about someone just come to me. They occur as if I had heard them before.

"Many psychics are psychopaths. I do not look for miracles—only the action and the reaction. Too many spiritualists are fanatics. Too many of those who follow

'isms' (spiritualism) really suffer 'asms' (spasms). If someone goes to a medium and then comes back and tells me
about how amazing the 'reading' was, I ask him a few
questions and frequently learn that he did most of the
talking and the medium then told him the same material
back. Such people are usually told what they want to hear.

"In 'spirit reading' you do not communicate with the
dead. You only pick up their vibrations from the past that
continually bombard us. The finite within us cannot communicate with the infinite, yet identity is never lost. The
Spiritual is a life within us that we cannot understand. Yet,
I can become aware of things that happened to them
(people who died) during their lifetime. The events usually had an emotional tone to them, something that ir-
ritated these persons or brought about a change or threatened change in their health, wealth, and popularity."

While Romano was in charge of the Eastman Kodak
exhibition at the Buffalo World's Fair in 1901, he had
one of his first experiences with a professional mind
reader, a Professor Zancigs. The "medium" was on the
platform and the professor in the audience. Mr. Romano
handed his card to the professor, and the "medium," after
a little hesitation, spelled out the name "Jacques Romano." Later, Romano became acquainted with the professor, who took a liking to him. The professor asked if
he would like to learn the "mind reading" act. He advised
Romano to get a woman "medium" with a good musical
ear. He said a medium must know your voice very well.
For instance, when the professor asked questions of the
"medium" on the stage, the particular tone of his voice
for the key word, 1, 2, 3, etc., had the specific letter, number, or code involved in the answer. Romano recalled, for
example, that the professor held a ring of keys that be-

longed to a member of the audience in the back of the
auditorium. When the professor asked the "medium" on
the stage how many keys were in the ring, she quickly
said eight. Eight was the exact number of words the
professor used in asking the question.

The more widely he traveled and the more carefully he
scrutinized his fellow man, the more certain Romano became that "miracles are just nature's law." He was always
interested in miracles and, accordingly, he studied magic
work and card tricks. In addition to the form of trickery
used by Professor Zancigs, Romano knew many other
types of collusion, card tricks, gadgets, and props. For
example, a famous "swami" had a "clairvoyant act" which
was really based on his superb vision and the manner in
which clay packs and bandages were applied to his forehead. The swami then readjusted the facial packs by
wrinkling his oily forehead in his pretrial adjustment.
Then through an almost unnoticeable peephole the
swami used his superb vision for the trick of spurious
clairvoyant reading ability.

When asked how he did many of his own card stunts,
such as correctly naming the card that he told a guest to
think of, Romano said it was a faculty or suggestion he
himself often did not understand. As an example, "I once
made a man shuffle the deck of cards, look at one in
private, reshuffle them, and put them in my pocket while
thinking of the card. I put my hand in the pocket and
pulled it out. I was more surprised than he."

In his reminiscences Romano recalled many of his own
psychic experiences. Once at the turn of the century, when
traveling for Eastman Kodak, he was to take a boat to
Kingston, Jamaica, to meet a customer. However, at the
last moment he had a presentiment and therefore missed

the boat. "When I arrived, I found out that there had been an earthquake and the man I was supposed to visit had been pinned under the beams. They had freed him by amputating his arm."

On another occasion Romano was ready to embark on a boat to Venezuela. This time he had a strange feeling that he should leave the boat immediately and return to his hotel room. He did, and found a telegram from his company warning him not to go to Venezuela as originally planned because of a smallpox epidemic. He just managed to unload all his belongings from the boat before it sailed.

"In Santos, Brazil, about 1905, I was sleeping in a hotel room but I was very restless. This was unusual for me, but everything has a cause and effect. It had been my custom always to visit an apartment or a house for a close friend before he would rent it. If the place was happy it permeated the walls; if it had held bitterness, I could quickly feel it. Anyway, in the Santos Hotel I went downstairs, talked to the clerk, and asked him, 'How is the smallpox around here?' He said, 'Oh, it's not too bad, but three weeks ago the man who was staying in your room died of it.'"

On another occasion Romano ". . . had to take a train to Charlottesville, Virginia, but shortly before the train was scheduled to leave, I felt noise (synesthesia) and saw a trestle burning. I did not take the train, but returned to the hotel. Later, I learned that the bridge [at the time the train passed over it] had burned down and many people had been killed.

"Once I was riding on the train next to a stranger whom I had seen commuting previously. I told him of my feeling that something had happened to his wife, that she wasn't well, and that he should get off the train at once. He said he had no reason to believe she was not well, and he behaved as though my presentiment was an uncalled for and reprehensible intrusion. However, when I met him later he said his wife had died when I had my premonition!

"I was connected with the John Hays Hammond Enterprises. One day I opened the door to Mr. Harris Hammond's office and noticed that he was busy with the man who was responsible for obtaining the oil leases in Mexico. When his visitor, Captain Ricardo Mestre, left, I asked Mr. Hammond what was wrong with the gentleman, because he looked as if he were almost dead. Mr. Hammond laughed and said, 'What's the matter with you? He's in the best of health and quite a tennis athlete. He's in the best of health!' The next day I learned that this man had died during the night.

"In 1910 I was in Cuba and attended a special dinner. Mrs. Richard Harding Davis, the 'Yama Yama' girl, was there. Among the other six guests I became acquainted with was a man who was an executive for a big copra company in New York. I did not see him again until 1920, during Prohibition, when I noticed him at a party. In his conversation, he told me how they extract lanolin from wool in Australia. Then, one day many years later, I wondered what had happened to him, because I recalled how this man knew the technique of extracting lanolin from sheep's wool; and at that moment I needed this knowledge for a product I was making. Three days later a tramp came to see me and ask my help. Formerly a respectable citizen, the tramp had become interested in psychic work, taken to drinking, and then his mind went all to pieces. That tramp was the copra executive of long ago, who had crossed my path and thoughts twice previously in my life.

"In 1912 Mrs. Stuyvesant Fish was a leader of the Four Hundred. She was an old woman at the time and very aggressive. One evening I told her that I had to leave and she said, 'If you go now you can never come back. So you had better stay.' She was very interested in John Jacob Astor, who had recently married for the second time. I told Mrs. Fish's fortune and along the way said that John Jacob Astor and his young wife would be in a different situation. I said, 'Don't worry about the marriage of John Jacob Astor; in one month he will be relieved—something will happen to him.' Mrs. Fish was concerned because, if something happened to John Jacob Astor, she'd be number one on the society map. One month later John Jacob Astor went down with the *Titanic*.

"At a dinner party in Pittsburgh in 1915, during World War I, I made a hit with John Hays Hammond by putting a newspaper man under hypnosis. By traveling clairvoyance I had the reporter go to the front and witness a battle at a certain bridge between the Italians and the Austrians. He correctly described the bridge, geographic points, and other events, which were all confirmed the next day in the newspapers.

"Another example (of traveling clairvoyance) occurred when a lawyer by the name of Sullivan, in Rochester, had to take care of Molly's divorce proceedings. Molly's husband was a rich businessman who lived on 86th Street in New York City. He traveled all over the country in his work, and we did not know where to serve the papers. Fortunately, I had a friend by the name of Pinky, a YMCA boy, in Rochester, whom I used in hypnotic work. I hypnotized Pinky, and when he was in a deep trance, my wife gave him her address in New York. Pinky then 'went' up to the house and said that 'three men are there playing bridge. One is a dummy and they bought the fourth hand.' Pinky said how strange the whole place was because it had many ornate rugs, some of which were hanging from the walls. This was interesting because my wife's husband was very fond of Persian rugs. Pinky next accurately described Molly's husband, and we knew that he was there. The lawyer then phoned an officer in New York, who served the papers on the husband the next day.

"On another occasion, when I was working with Pinky, we went to visit the home of a Mr. Osborn, a close friend of Mr. Smith, the Grand Master of the Masonic Lodge of New York State. There were thirty-five to forty guests at his home. Before proceeding with the traveling clairvoyance, I put Pinky in a trance and told the audience that Pinky could sometimes predict when different people would die. When I asked for suggestions from the audience, John D. Rockefeller was mentioned. However, this would not do, so I asked Pinky about Mrs. Rockefeller. He predicted the exact date of her death, which occurred sometime later in the year of our séance (March 15, 1915). Then, Grand Master Smith asked me if Pinky would tell him what his father was doing in Yaphank, Long Island. I said: Give me the address and house number. While Pinky was still in a trance I 'sent' him over. Now my Mason friend, Mr. Smith, weighed more than two hundred pounds, was short, about five feet, seven inches, and baldheaded. I had an idea that his father would be something like him. Pinky 'went' to the house, but he said he could not see anyone. Then he noticed a light in the back room, and he spotted a woman reading a newspaper. It was the maid. He also described the porch upstairs and the arrangement of the room. Pinky looked into the bedroom and saw a man asleep. Because of Mr. Smith's short and rotund physique, I figured that his father would be somewhat the same. Pinky surprised us by saying, 'What a tall man! He's well over six feet tall. Why—his feet are sticking out over the bed! And he has lots of hair!' The audience gasped in amazement and then exploded into laughter, because many of them knew Mr. Smith's father was six feet, four inches, tall and had a bushy head of hair for an old man!"

Although Romano raised money for the United States in World War I by selling Liberty Bonds and appearing at benefits as a "palmist," he was busy in other spheres also. "In the first global war I was consulted by the Secret Service. I had a hunch that the enemy was getting messages out of the country by writing on chocolates. I suspected that they used a salt solution. When the chocolates were sent to Spain, they were sprayed with a chemical solution and black writing became legible. The hunch proved to be correct. On one other occasion, during World War I, I had a hunch that the German Rotograph Company was sending out coded messages by the specific order in which the pictures of the American pin-up girls were packed. This also was confirmed."

Unofficially the government made further use of Romano's psychic-sleuthing talents. "Downstairs was a saloon and upstairs they caught a German who was allegedly signaling a German submarine by raising and lowering the window shade. Two detectives caught him and locked him up. He was brought to League Island, Philadelphia. They could not reach Milliken, who was the high chief, so they asked me to examine him. I looked at him and said 'Let him go. He is innocent. But there is an Irish woman there who hates the United States and falsely accused this man.'

"They verified my statements, for it developed that the wind blew the shade, and this accounted for the 'signaling.' When I shook the German's hand, I noticed that he had thick callouses, and it appeared to me unlikely that he would be a spy. Later they found the Irish woman and had to lock her up. She hated the English and was a Sinn Feiner.

"Another episode occurred when I was at League Island and shook hands with a new Commander who was introduced to me by the head man. Later I told the chief that the new Commander and his secretary were working against him. I told the Chief that the Commander, contrary to what he claimed, really used to follow married men and women, as a private detective, and that he used to go to circuses and carnivals to play the shell game. However, the clincher was when I told the Chief to watch out for a delay in some important personal papers, and that we would soon receive some unfavorable information from Washington about the new Commander. Three weeks later this came about. Five months later, when I returned to League Island, I learned from my friend, the Chief, that an investigation of my statements was successfully carried out and that after subsequent events they had to get rid of the Commander."

Harold Sherman, the noted author and psychic researcher, was a close friend of Romano's for many years, and wrote in many articles about his unusual experiences with Romano. He gave generous credit to Romano in *Thoughts Through Space,* a book about telepathic communications between the North Pole explorer, Sir Hubert Wilkins, and Harold Sherman. He also dedicated an earlier fictional work, a boy's adventure story, to "Jacques Romano—as fine a friend as man could have . . ."

(*Tahara in the Land of Yucatan,* Goldsmith Publishing Co., Chicago, 1933).

Sherman's article in *Fate* magazine, September, 1960, describes some extraordinary telepathic feats. He told how in the 1920's Romano once lectured and entertained 125 young men. When he finished, his host, Mr. Bill, remarked that the lecture was so interesting he had forgotten about the time and had missed his 10:00 P.M. train out of Grand Central Station. Romano nonchalantly told him not to worry because there was a delay: "The train did not leave Grand Central Station until 10:20 and there had been a wreck out around Mamaroneck—it is still being held at the 125th Street Station." Mr. Bill and the other men who were present thought that Romano was completely wrong and carried away with himself, as that particular train was seldom or never late. However, because of Romano's unshakable self-confidence, Mr. Bill phoned Grand Central Station and then returned to the party completely flabbergasted. "My God, it is delayed, and for the first time in fifteen years! Some freight trains collided out near Mamaroneck and all the traffic has been held up. My train is no further than the 125th Street Station at 2:00 A.M.!"

A long-time personal friend of Romano's was Frederick C. Heyer, Ph.D., of the Charles Scriven Printing Company in New York City. He was interviewed in his office and recalled many interesting personal experiences. Dr. Heyer had kept a file on Romano for many years. "I met Dr. Romano in 1921, September, it was. In those days he was close to sixty. He bragged about the fact! I met him in connection with New York University, at one of their dinners at which he was a guest speaker. Then, one day in the fall of 1922, Doc called me up at the office and said he had to talk to me. I told him I would miss my train and that I was on my way to an athletic event. Doc said, 'You are too much of a gentleman to hang up on me.' He persisted in talking, and in fact tied me up so long that I missed the train. He talked about generalities. It was irritating, because he was detaining me. He didn't know at the time why he was detaining me, but only that he had to. The Lehigh Valley Black Diamond Flyer, the train I was supposed to take, was wrecked, and all my companions who left before I did were killed or injured. Nine men died in the train and three men a little later. Doc saved my life!

"I lost track of him for six or seven years. In October, 1928, I met him downtown. He said, 'Give me your phone number, I'll call you up sometime.' Six months later, 'Have you got any money in the stock market? Sell it!' I thought he was crazy. Later I lost everything I had. I 'phoned him when I found out about the crash. His many suggestions to business executives, over the years, have been a constant source of amazement to me. I have been in his office many times when an executive of a large concern called to ask for his advice.

"In 1931–1933 we saw quite a bit of each other. One day, Dr. Romano met a man called Heilman in my office, for a brief moment. Heilman was business manager for the Brooklyn State Hospital. For some reason Romano became very upset. I thought he was ill. When Heilman left, Doc said to me, 'You're supposed to go to dinner tomorrow night? Don't go. I'll call you at 7 o'clock.' I did not go to the dinner and gave my ticket to an associate. The man to whom I gave the ticket telephoned the following night about 6:30 P.M. to say that Heilman had dropped dead at the bar. Romano called at 7:00 P.M. 'You knew that Heilman dropped dead? I saw the angel of death around him!'

"Romano predicted Mussolini's apprehension. At the time (Sunday, July 11, 1943), Romano was at a party in the company of Mr. and Mrs. Denis P. S. Conan Doyle (the son of Sir Arthur Conan Doyle, author of *Sherlock Holmes*), the Duchess de Talleyrand, Princess Nina Mdvani, Lady Montague, and Madame Yen. In the course of a conversation on psychic phenomena Romano told the guests, 'I just felt something. One week from now you will hear it on the radio, Sunday, July 18th, between 9:00 and 10:00 A.M. There will be an announcement of Mussolini's arrest by the Italian government.' It happened just as he said. The news came over the radio about 9:30 A.M. on the 18th of July, 1943. He felt the plotters and knew it would happen."

This prediction was confirmed in a letter from Denis P. S. Conan Doyle ("I recall very well your July 11, 1943, remarkably accurate prophecy, the extraordinary fulfill-ment of which, even to the date, is indeed a testimonial to your remarkable powers."), a memorandum of Ro-mano's written at the time, and a personal interview with Madame Yen.

Dr. Heyer continued, "I had a place in the country and would go there on weekends. I'd be talking about Romano to my guests and then he'd call me up on Monday and say 'You've been talking about me.' Once, I got a letter from relatives in Europe asking for money. Romano, who had no knowledge of the letter, called me and said, 'Forget about it; they have plenty of money.' It later developed that he was right.

"Alvin Brunet had never met Dr. Romano before, but he was told 'when you were twelve a horse kicked you.

You have the scars on your leg . . . the worst thing they ever did to your wife was radium treatment—the cancer never would have spread.' Brunet was dumbfounded.

"A Russian nobleman, Nicholas D'Assorgioff, a sponge who tried to get everything he could, was in the habit of ridiculing anything, anyone, and at any time. Romano, who never cared much for personal appearances, had on a battered old fedora which looked as if it had been worn through the Civil War. When he entered the room, D'Assorgioff ridiculed him: 'I have my doubts about anyone who would wear a hat like that!' Romano turned, looked at him, and said, 'My dear fellow, when you get home, see if you can find that hat you now wear!' By the time D'Assorgioff got home, he had no hat, and until his death, the $50 Borsalino hat that he had been so proud of had not been found.

"Another time, many years ago, I had engaged Dr. Romano's services for a lecture and he benefited someone in the audience. After I introduced him he went out on the stage, put his hands in his pockets, and walked up and down. He said, 'There's a man here in great danger! He is supposed to undergo an operation for stomach ulcers tomorrow. You haven't got ulcers. You have ulcerated teeth! There is a dentist waiting to take three of your teeth out.' The man went to the dentist, had the teeth pulled and never had the operation or was further troubled with his stomach. He died last week at eighty-three years of age."

Dr. Heyer continued, "I happen to be an adopted member of the Algonquin Indian tribe. This tribe also adopted Romano. He once told the Indian chief about many things that had transpired in his life. Romano seems to be able to work this 'mind reading' with any person. He can also take on uncooperative people and be successful. He told Mrs. Charles Garrett that she was an artist and he asked her to draw a crooked line. Romano said that he saw four faces in her crooked line. He then asked Mrs. Garrett to give him the pencil—but she couldn't let go of it. Finally, in some mysterious way, Romano influenced her and she was able to release the pencil and put it down on the table. Romano then said that the pencil would have to come to him. He put his hand on the table and the pencil rolled over to him. There was another woman whom he hypnotized and through her produced raps on the table or wall. He always denied any supernatural explanation for these phenomena even though he claimed that he did not know how he did it.

"He was lecturing at the Masonic Temple and doing card tricks. One man dropped a card and Romano picked it up and stuck it in his pocket. Since I had seen him with this card phenomenon many times, but had never seen him do that before, I remembered this and wondered why. The man who dropped the card died several days after the meeting. Later, I asked Romano why he picked up that card and he said he did not know.

"When I [Dr. Heyer] was five, I was shot in the head with a .22 caliber rifle. The bullet lodged there and stayed for a number of years. I went to the Mayo Clinic for a diagnosis. They said that if they removed the bullet my vision would probably be destroyed. Years later I went to Johns Hopkins, and they also said that any surgery might cost me my sight. Still another specialist said I would lose my sight. So the bullet stayed there. Romano told me that the bullet would come out by itself, and not to worry about it. A number of years later, when I was puttering around in the attic I hit my head on the beams. The blow cracked the casing around the bullet. I went to my family doctor, and when he pulled the bullet out, it was pulverized.

"Romano is very proud. He won't let anyone take over his business. He came over on a Monday. 'Business is lousy.' I asked him if he wanted some money. 'No, by Thursday business will be better. My friends won't forget me.' He called me on Thursday; he had received a substantial check in the mail.

"On numerous occasions he told people of things they had done in the distant past and forgotten about, of scars on different parts of their bodies, and so forth. When he first met my wife he told her things that she had heard her great grandfather talk about, and also about a brother of her grandfather's who was a Civil War veteran.

"He used to come up to the country to visit us. Then one day he said that he did not want me to invite him any more, because 'You'll have a lot of trouble if she (Mrs. Romano) dies up here in bed.' He called me up when his wife died and said, 'I feel so all alone.'

"Once years ago I wrote a letter to the *Reader's Digest* thinking they would be interested in Romano as 'The Most Unforgettable Character I Have Ever Known' and I got back a letter inquiring if I knew what I was talking about!"

*   *   *

Another old friend, Louis Zara, the noted prize-winning author, had recorded his first meeting with Romano. It was in 1942 in Chicago. "I met Jacques Romano at approximately 11:30 A.M. in the Fine Arts Building. With him were Mr. and Mrs. Harold Sherman and Mr. Sherman's mother, who had come in from Marion, Indiana, for the holiday season. After the introductions, Mr. Sherman pointed out that the Piccadilly Tea Room, where we had expected to lunch, was closed that day. We thereupon decided to go to the La Salle Street Station and lunch in the depot restaurant. Upon Mrs. Zara's arrival we drove to the station and subsequently had our luncheon at the Gateway Restaurant.

"From the moment of our introduction Mr. Romano began a lively conversation that fairly sparkled with witty remarks. As I later thought about it, he seemed to be laying down a barrage of repartee while he busily probed every new mind he encountered. Once our lunch was ordered, Mr. Sherman remarked casually, 'Jacques, did you get any impression of Mr. Zara when you met him and shook hands?' Mr. Romano nodded and began to give his impressions.

"What was most startling about these impressions was the swiftness with which they were delivered. No fumbling, no groping for words, but sharp, concise statements, almost as though he were reading written records. As far as I could observe, in the midst of my increasing astonishment at his accuracy, he made no attempt to eye me and simply went ahead, confident that what he was saying was the truth. As Mrs. Zara and I registered amazement and corroborated the truth of his statements, he seemed to warm to his subject and went on. At times his impressions came so swiftly that I had barely the space in which to register one impression when he was already talking of another.

"It must be stated that nearly all of the impressions which he uttered were not known to the Shermans, whose acquaintance we had but recently made. It must also be added that Mr. Romano seemed to avoid those fixed dates,

such as birth, schooling, marriage, etc., which are easily
ascertainable from *Who's Who.*

"I should also add that I had never had an experience
of this sort before and that I regard it as certainly the most
unusual meeting I have ever had with any human being.
What impressed me, even more than his ability to probe
into my own past, was the apparent ease with which he
picked up my father's story. If I were to attempt a ra-
tionalization, I can only say that I have always been deeply
tied up emotionally with my father, and with his well-
being, but how Mr. Romano got that and the corollary
facts, many of which were unknown even to me, I do not
know. In the entire meeting the only statement which
Mr. Romano made which I have, thus far, been unable
to corroborate was one concerning Africa and Johannes-
burg. It seems to me that one would be grudging to say
that Mr. Romano, in this instance, had attained an average
of only about 96 per cent accuracy!"

MEMO ON JACQUES ROMANO'S IMPRESSIONS OF LOUIS ZARA
DECEMBER 24, 1942
GATEWAY RESTAURANT, LA SALLE STREET STATION,
CHICAGO, ILLINOIS

IMPRESSION	CORROBORATION
Mr. Romano: I see you at eighteen or nineteen having something to do with laws —reading or studying.	After finishing high school, Louis Zara worked for seven years in the print shop of a lawbook publishing concern.
Mr. Romano: Was there a name like Helen in connec-	The name of this concern was The Callaghan Pub-

IMPRESSION	CORROBORATION
tion with this place? Helen —no, Harriet—no, Helen —no, Kellen or Callen?	lishing Co.
Mr. Romano: I see an office with a sofa, and a man who has fallen and others carrying him out.	While working during the hot weather, the vice president of the company collapsed from the heat, and Louis Zara called responsible persons to have him taken to the hospital.
Mr. Romano: I don't know what you do, but it seems to me you do two or three jobs instead of only one.	In addition to his own writing and his post as editorial consultant at *Esquire*, Louis Zara was Executive Director of the Chicago Office of Russian War Relief, Inc.
Mr. Romano: In 1932 something happened which seemed to set your career definitely in the right direction. In 1933 and 1934 you were somewhat uncertain, but by 1935 you were definitely established in your profession.	In 1932, H. L. Mencken published Louis Zara's first short story and in the next two years his first novel, *Blessed Is the Man,* was written, published, and favorably received.
Mr. Romano: Did your father have a brother who ran away from home? I get an impression of Johannesburg in South Africa.	Although Louis Zara did not know it, having always had the impression that his father was an only son, his father had many brothers.

IMPRESSION

CORROBORATION

(This fact was subsequently supplied by his father.) However, his father was the youngest in a large family and, although he knows that several of his brothers died while young, he cannot say for certain that there was or was not a brother who ran away from home.

Mr. Romano: Did your father have a brother or someone very close to him who dropped dead suddenly?

Subsequent checkup with Louis Zara's father brought to light the fact that his father had a brother-in-law who died in exactly this manner.

Mr. Romano: I see your father. He has a habit of running his forefinger along the side of his nose and nostril.

True. Louis Zara's father had a tear gland removed in an eye operation and since then uses this gesture to brush away the outside of the passages near the nose.

Mr. Romano: Your father has a severe pain in his side. He strained himself while lifting something and has suffered this pain ever since. He also has some trouble with his teeth, particularly in the lower jaw on the right-hand side, where bad

True. Louis Zara's father had suffered this hernia for a good many years. The teeth facts are also completely accurate, and he recently underwent dental treatment.

IMPRESSION	CORROBORATION

teeth and the space between them are causing trouble.

Mr. Romano: Your father made quite a decisive move in 1900. For about six months, everything was uncertain, then things seemed to settle down. He has a scar or a mark on his chin.

In 1900 Louis Zara's father entered the Russian army. He developed some sort of growth on the side of his neck, and went through a very painful operation without anesthesia. In the ensuing months he was shifted from one branch of the service to another and was not permanently settled for about six months. (The scar is on the back of his neck, behind the ear.)

Mr. Romano: The years 1914 to 1916 were unsettled times for your father. I see some moving around and then in 1916, quite a shift, in which furniture and household goods were lost.

Louis Zara's father moved from New York City to Buffalo and, after some uncertain times there, moved to Chicago in 1916. Much of the furniture and household goods was smashed and broken on the trip.

Mr. Romano: To get back to more recent times. About four or five years ago you were in a place about 175 miles from here in that direction (pointing northeast). It isn't a town and I

From May to September, 1938, Louis Zara and his family lived in Michigan, in a little town called Port Sheldon, 176 miles from Chicago. (The place was not really a town, just a

IMPRESSION	CORROBORATION
can't see it clearly, but it has a two-word name.	collection of summer cottages strung out along the lake.)
Mr. Romano: I get an impression of a real estate deal, involving a two-story building. There is talk of much-needed repairs on the first floor and the roof of the building seems to be leaking, for on the ceiling of the living room is a large damp spot which never quite dries.	On December 20, the previous Sunday, some prospective buyers of the apartment in which Louis Zara lives came to see the apartment. The man who was interested in purchasing the building, an architect (and incidentally a man who had been a schoolmate of Louis Zara's), remarked on the wet spot in the ceiling and stated the reason for it.
Mr. Romano: In about September of this year you were offered a reorganization job with a firm of magazine publishers or book publishers.	In the early fall, the Ziff-Davis Publishing Company offered Louis Zara the managing editorship of their book division, which was a new venture, an outgrowth of their magazine publishing business.
Mr. Romano: On Monday at 4:00 P.M. I see you working at your desk. You receive a telephone call which upsets you greatly, and which seems to necessitate considerable readjustment	*At exactly* 4:00 P.M. on Monday, Louis Zara received a call from one of the Board of Directors of Russian War Relief, for which he acted as Executive Director. The information

IMPRESSION CORROBORATION

in the work you are doing. he received upset him considerably, inasmuch as it
concerned the carrying out
of a program in which he
believed.

Mr. Zara dedicated his book *Rebel Run* (Crown Publishers, New York, 1951) to Romano.

"In our initial conversation, when there was no reason
that he knew the least thing about me or my background,
he immediately picked up various thoughts about my
father and described experiences which I, myself, did not
know about the man, about things that had happened to
him forty years earlier when he was a soldier in Russia. As
you may understand, I was deeply involved emotionally
with my own father, and perhaps, naturally, would be assumed to give off 'vibrations,' if such a thing does exist.
How Romano, sitting and facing me, could manage to be
able to tell me things about which I knew nothing—including the fact that my father, whom I had always
thought an only son, had had a brother who had gotten
lost years ago—I will never know. For whatever it may
be worth, I can testify that this actually happened. He
also described emotional experiences of my own; for example, that at one time I had fallen down a staircase in
a print shop where I worked as a boy while going to college. He seemed to be able to tap the wells of my own
memory. I know that there are many instances, when he
first begins to talk to a person, when he merely relies on
his shrewd judgment as an observer of the human animal.
But, I must also add that much of what he has said is far,
far beyond anything like that. He simply is able to make

contact with thoughts and emotions which, to the naked eye, lie buried behind the forehead of the person whom he is addressing.

"If I told you that on December 24, 1942, when the Russian armies had their backs to the wall in Stalingrad, this man predicted the remarkable victories which followed two months later, practically giving me the precise dates when the victories would take place and when they would be announced, would you believe me? I would not expect you to believe me at all. Yet the fact is that on that day I told other people of his prediction, and everyone laughed about it. Yet subsequently, as is now history, those victories did take place, and the German armies were smashed.

"I could go on and on and recite dozens of experiences that I have had with him, or that I have witnessed, or that I have had from hearsay from others. I am not naive. I know that in the midst of all these remarkable gifts he also is able to employ an unusual talent for assessing the other person's personality and for reaching conclusions that seemed to be closed to ordinary persons like myself. He only knows that he has these powers, that they have worked for him through the years, and that he has never done anyone any harm by them."

Another long-time friend, Judge John Warren Hill of New York City, kindly wrote about some of his experiences through the years:

"I have known of Jacques Romano since about 1902–1903 when as a small boy I heard my father speak of him. My father was Reverend Dr. John Wesley Hill, a very well-known public figure. He was in 1896–1902 a very good friend of President McKinley and Mark Hanna, who was a U.S. Senator and McKinley's closest friend.

"Around 1902, at breakfast or dinner, my father recounted an experience he had had with a man in Hanna's office the day before. This man had done some curious things, then told my father to write a name on a piece of paper, and then he had left the room. Father said he wrote the name of his mother 'Elizabeth' on a piece of paper while this man was out of the room. On his return he told my father, 'The name you wrote was Elizabeth.'

"About six years later my father brought this man to our home and told me it was the man he had met in Hanna's office a number of years before. He retold the above experience to my stepmother, my father having lost my mother and remarried since then. That man was Jacques Romano. Today, I know him well.

"I would say that when I met Romano, around 1908 or 1909, he was *at least* the same age as my father, who was then forty-five or forty-seven (depending on year of this visit). Romano always looked much younger than his actual age. I would say that today [1960] Romano is around one hundred years of age.

"I have heard tell of many strange clairvoyant demonstrations he has made. Dr. Milton Bridger, a very well-known diagnostician of Post Graduate Hospital, met Romano through me. He did not believe Romano controlled his pulse beat to make it stop. Before he died, Dr. Bridger told me that he and Dr. Dannreuther (one time president of the New York County Medical Association) had Romano in Bridger's office and had observed his heart under the fluoroscope and that Romano's heart had stopped.*

"One night at my home, several years ago, Romano

* Romano's extraordinary hypnotic abilities suggest, as one reasonable hypothesis, that he had the two physicians under his spell and they were hallucinated. For example, a Detroit newspaper clipping of 1915 stated: "Dr. J. B. Kennedy examined a man under the spell of Romano and declared that his left pulse had stopped entirely. 'It's beyond me,' he said."

said to one of my guests (whom he had never heard of or met before), 'Think of a name.' The guest thought of the name of a woman, his mother. Romano said, 'I see the letters C — R — A —, the name is Clara,' and the name was Clara."

Mrs. Bessie Mitchell Boehm, of New York City, who knew Jacques Romano years ago and then met him again in 1959 after noticing the *New Yorker* magazine (July 19, 1958, pp. 21–22) article about him, wrote:

"It was during the year 1911 that I first met Mr. Romano at a party and he escorted me home. When we arrived home I told my mother what a wonderful gentleman he was and all the things he could do, so he showed my mother a few of the things. After that Mr. Romano became a close friend of the family.

"At that time Mr. Romano was connected with the manufacturing of the Bleriot Monoplane, as manager. My mother belonged to many clubs, at that time, and Mr. Romano entertained at many of them.

"At the time of meeting Mr. Romano, I was sixteen years old and Mr. Romano was then about forty-five. His youthfulness, combined with worldly experience, puzzled many of my family's friends. From various sources my family received information that Mr. Romano was about twenty-five when he came to the United States, in 1889.

"One phenomenon he produced was to have my mother (while in a hypnotic trance) without contact (hands, feet, etc.), knock on the wall, ceiling, tables, etc. Mr. Romano, in a calm sort of way, would tell my mother to knock on the table as many times as there were people in the room; the knocks would come accordingly.

"With the passing of time, Mr. Romano told my mother that she would be able to produce the knocking sounds without his help. It was my mother's pleasure, when she retired, to say goodnight to my dead brother, and immediately there was a knock on the bed's footboard.

"I must say Mr. Romano's hypnotic power was wonderful. I can well remember another time when he hypnotized my mother, and she wrote things from the spirit of my brother. We were able to find a box in a vault, after his death, which we knew nothing about.

"Another time I was in Massachusetts and I was doing a lot of sailing; I received a letter from my mother telling me to stop going out. I was sure she knew nothing about my sailing at the time, but the spirit of my brother had told her.

"Lately I read a newspaper article about Mr. Romano and I telephoned him. We met after forty years, I knew him at once; he seemed unchanged."

* * *

From letters in his possession and a personal interview, it appeared that Romano had correctly foretold the death of Madam Huang's (pseudonym) mother when her physicians, in October, had given her up as hopeless. Romano flaunted their advice with, "Don't worry. She will live now, but will die in the middle of February" (which was many months away).

He did a similar thing in another corroborated instance. He told the family of an elderly woman with diabetic gangrene that the surgeons should not amputate, that she would recover. The family followed Romano's risky advice and she recovered.

Although of great help to Madam Huang, Madame Kung, Madame Wellington Koo, and others, Romano never talked about his connections. He was well known to the Soong sisters, including Madame Chiang Kai-shek. She reputedly sought his advice while on private rides in a chauffeur-driven limousine, and at such times he received a chicken from her as a reward. This practice continued until he correctly foretold the collapse of Nationalist China.

Madame Huang recalled how during the Sino-Japanese War, "I had no contact with my daughter, my only child, for one year. She was expecting a baby. I was afraid that I had lost her. Romano was very nice in comforting me. He would phone and say, 'Don't worry, she's all right.' He then said, 'You'll hear from her.' And I did at approximately the time he said I would. The letter was routed through Chungking and was delivered by foot. He told me then, when I did not hear from her for a long time again, 'Don't worry, she's changing scenery. I see her on the sea. There is water around her.' Later on, I heard she had left Hong Kong by boat and was on her way to Shanghai. This was quite a surprise to us. He would tell me he saw it as clear as a picture. I was always astounded. I thought he was comforting me out of kindness, but he was always right. A letter in those days was a rare occurrence. I received one, if that often, only once every three or four months."

For Romano, serendipity was almost an everyday experience. People came, wrote, or phoned him with the necessary answers to problems in his daily life. For instance, "Shortly after World War I, I wanted to obtain a special razor manufactured in Germany, but I did not know where to go. Then, one day, for no good reason at all, I got off the subway at 59th Street and bumped into an old friend, who was flabbergasted at the coincidence, since he had been at that very moment looking for me. He wanted to introduce me to two German businessmen who were marketing socks. During the conversation the salesmen became interested in me, and one of them said, 'Would you like a nice razor?' It was the exact razor that I sought." On another occasion he could not develop the proper contrast on a photographic film. When he was stymied by this, he received a letter from a man in St. Louis who, although writing about an appointment for another matter, mentioned the particular chemicals that were needed for the film.

When Romano was in great need of money, a millionaire in the South whom he knew phoned him and said, "I was dreaming of you, Jacques, and I am sending you a check for $1,500." Once when the rents were going up in New York City, Romano became very worried about how he could possibly raise the money to keep his laboratory going. After Romano suffered through a half-hour's concern over how he could ever pay his landlord, the landlord knocked on the door and said, "It's a very funny thing, Mr. Romano, but I've been thinking a lot about you for the past half hour and, instead of raising your rent, I've decided to lower it!"

Frequently in the course of this study I phoned Romano only to have him answer by greeting me by name, before I spoke, and then say he had been thinking of me and expected the call. One winter day after a particularly heavy blizzard, I went into New York on other business. Arriving ahead of my appointment I decided to pay Mr. Romano a surprise call. But alas! He was at the door, which was half open. Apparently he had been expecting me all the time. Then, in private, I greeted Mrs. Romano, who had been ailing for many months, and she said that her husband had told her earlier that he thought I would visit him that day.

In an attempt to verify one of Romano's many extraordinary experiences, on Monday, February 17, 1958, I phoned the *Herald News* of Passaic, New Jersey, to check his alleged published prophecy of the death of William Randolph Hearst. The editor of the paper, Mr. McMahon, did not recall this event of a few years ago but suggested that I contact William M. McBride, who was the chief editor for thirty-five years and was then living in retirement. The next morning I succeeded in reaching McBride and asked, "What do you know about Jacques Romano?" He was much surprised that I should call him about such a matter since he had just finished reading the obituary of Romano's wife in the New York *Herald Tribune.*

McBride then recalled how at a party Romano had asked him to think of someone whom he knew well and was now dead. Romano then correctly described Mr. McBride's first cousin, a Franciscan monk, as a holy man with a (congenitally) twisted arm who had died a year before. Mr. Romano also correctly stated that at the time of the monk's death he was on a mission tour in Latin America. Romano produced this factual data without any previous knowledge of the monk, Mr. McBride, or anyone else at the party.

Before describing the Hearst incident, McBride referred to Arnold Chapel, a hearing aid specialist. Chapel stated that he once was dubious about taking a hearing aid booth during a convention at the Paterson Armory until Romano told him he would break even financially and have 1,300 visitors. The monetary outcome was as predicted, and when a tally was taken there were exactly 1,280 visitors. Chapel then discussed the Hearst prophecy: "Eddie Reardon, currently the Washington correspondent for the *Herald News,* Mr. McBride, two physicians, and I were together at a private party when Romano said that he had a peculiar feeling that William Randolph Hearst was going to die in not less than two weeks and not more than six weeks. Later, during the party, Mr. Romano stated that Mr. Hearst would die within six weeks. When I drove Mr. Romano home that night, he told me that Hearst would die on Wednesday, August 14th, and I told my wife this. Earlier that evening, at the party, a notation was made of Romano's two-to-six-weeks prediction, and a few days later the *Journal American* was contacted for the purpose of checking on Mr. Hearst's state of health. They said that Mr. Hearst was no worse and no better than he had been in the past two years, and that there was no reason to expect his imminent death." Several weeks later Chapel received a telephone call from McBride about a feature article on the editorial page.

THE HERALD NEWS, THURSDAY, AUGUST 15, 1957

Foreboding of Death

"Jacques Romano, 84-year-old chemical manufacturer, of 101 Maiden Lane, Manhattan, was a guest at the Spring Street home of Mr. and Mrs. Arnold Chaplitsky in Passaic on July 18, recounting his experiences among Arab tribesmen and devotees of Hindu yogi. Two physicians and two newspapermen were in the group that saw Mr. Romano stop his pulse and drain one hand of blood. He also gave a demonstration of telepathy. Ed Reardon related some incidents of the evening in a recent column written for this page.

"Several days after his visit, Mr. Romano told his Passaic host, 'Ask your newspaper friends to inquire, discreetly, if anything happened to Hearst, the publisher. This morning I had a feeling like a pain in my stomach but I had no pain. I began thinking of Hearst. I got the conviction that he would be dead within six weeks.' That was less than a month ago. Hearst executives in New York, to whom the incident was related, said they had heard no news of any change in the health of the master of San Simeon. William Randolph Hearst died Wednesday, August 14th, at 12:45 P.M. New York time."

During Christmas, 1960, in Montclair, New Jersey, Jacques Romano told John B. Peterson, a Minneapolis contractor, that he need not ". . . worry because Kennedy would never run again in 1964 because he wouldn't be around." Miss Borghild Ericson of New York City was also a witness to this unusual statement. Peterson said later, "The minute I heard the news of President Kennedy's assassination (on the auto radio)—the old man— Jacques Romano—flashed into my mind."

Although many of these unusual experiences could not be further documented, they should not be uncritically rejected. There is, in fact, genuine value in recording them, because, in conjunction with the material on psychic experiments (Chapter 13), some pattern may be discerned and clues uncovered about the mechanism of this strange faculty, called by some an occult power. The observations, convictions, and experiences of such a man might have many indirect connections with his occult abilities. If, as is likely, the emotional elements are significant, any material, even subjective data, on the experiences, opinions, and philosophy of such a unique person as Jacques Romano might open new vistas leading to discoveries yet undreamed.

XI

USING PSYCHIC AWARENESS
IN EVERYDAY LIVING

*"He looked at me intently and began reading my mind
so revealingly that I nervously asked Mr. Romano to
please read to himself."*

—ED WALLACE, *New York World Telegram,*
APRIL 19, 1941

NAME any outstanding psychic personality or think of
any mental feat performed in the past fifty years, and
the chances are that Romano either knew the person or
could perform the feat himself. As he recalled his experiences throughout the years, the narratives varied little,
point for point.

Romano was unorthodox, but highly effective. Some of
his best adventures were vividly remembered by those who
took part in them. The following selected anecdotes give
a further insight into Romano himself; how his telepathic
abilities often left him more surprised than his audience,
and how he was nothing if not versatile.

THE GREATEST PSYCHICS

"Mr. Romano, who is the greatest psychic you have ever
known? Would it be Eusapia Palladino, Edgar Cayce,
Arthur Ford?"

"No. It was someone who lived in a cave and could trace people over great distances. He must have had great powers of observation. I have never found anyone as sensitive as he. Once I asked him how he did it and he said, 'I just sense it; you see, I'm a bloodhound.' "

MADAME BLAVATSKY

"In England, in 1887, I met Madame Blavatsky, who was lecturing. We conversed in French and English. She also knew Hindustani. In those days I could do mind reading much faster than today. My friend brought me to see her to get her opinion about me. She told my friend that I was an advanced soul. She asked a number of questions and then said, 'Now, you are one who will understand my theory about reincarnation. When one reaches avatar (highest of elements), you are born and nothing will disturb you.' She said that in time I would find this out. I could never accept her ideas on reincarnation, nor the Hindu belief that if one killed an animal it might be his grandfather or someone else. It is strange, but nothing disturbed me at the time I met Madame Blavatsky and nothing has since. When you meet someone great, you talk for a very short period, because you both know the same things and there's no reason for talking."

COUÉ AND GURDJIEFF

"I met Coué and Gurdjieff at Fontainebleau. Coué was originally a druggist, who later gained great fame as a healer. His methods were based on suggestion, and he emphasized how health could be obtained through self-help. However, in my opinion, his popular slogan, 'Every day in every way I'm getting better and better,' was about as useful as kissing the Blarney Stone. By having people say this, Coué really implanted the idea that they were sick yesterday and now they were busy driving it away with suggestive incantations. Thus, he did as much to make people conscious of ill health and worries as he did to help them. There is no better example of this than Coué himself. By 'curing' so many people, he gradually became so sympathetic toward their ailments that he actually absorbed many of their complaints and died a horrible death from autosuggestion!

"Whereas Coué became so involved in his work and the associated fanfare that he succumbed to it, Gurdjieff was a healthy man and a great teacher who could hypnotize many people at once. In his work he used hypnotic suggestion to perfect extraordinary dancing techniques of split-second timing. Gurdjieff got much enjoyment out of his work and thrived in a state of superb health."

THE WALDORF-ASTORIA

Paul Brunton, the well-known English writer on Hindu Yoga, told Romano about "the great master who spent sixteen years in a cave meditating." He described how the Yogi spoke in a soft monotone and how the cave where he lived was drab and without coloring. He emphasized the fact that the climatic conditions were the same throughout the year and thus favorably influenced his progression in Yoga.

Romano commented: "So that's what he needed to become a Yogi. My experience is quite different. If a man believes in the supreme power that originally made the four seasons of the year, that are all interwoven, that spring follows winter and the warm day can become a cold day, and that climatic conditions can always change, this man, then, will be able to take advantage of the situation and act as though these climatic changes were made for his benefit. For instance, the changes in weather favor my developing a resistance to disease so that I can stay healthy.

"You say that a Yogi, in order to concentrate on a subject, must be able to eliminate everything extraneous from his mind and retire into a trancelike state in his cave. Why don't you and I go over to a ball at the Waldorf-Astoria some day, where the bands are playing? Then you can ask me a question and, despite all the blaring music, I will not hear or see any of the noisemakers. I will not be distracted by this. If you don't say anything and are quiet, I will give you the answer without having to go into a corner and hide myself. The Yogis secrete themselves from Nature in order to favor their meditation, but I have been in all Nature's elements—in Siberia when it was 60° below zero, and in the sun near the equator in South America at 135°. My experience tells me that to be a Yogi in India is one thing, but it is quite another thing for a Westerner to achieve. Both of us, the Yogi and I, can attain similar goals, but only by being true to our own traditions and conceptions of supreme power."

A MANHATTAN SEANCE

"There was quite a gay and noisy party at a swank Sutton Place, New York, apartment. Among those present were many theatrical people, including Fanny Brice

('Baby Snooks') and Beatrice Lillie. Fanny Brice was sitting on the couch with four other people. I arrived a little late. The man sitting next to Fanny nudged me, 'Tell me something; tell me something!' I did not know who he was and felt rather uncomfortable at his dictatorial manner. I said that I did not feel like it. However, he was so insistent that I turned around and said, 'What was the matter with the man who was supposed to go to Buenos Aires on a special mission for you and then backed out?' He recoiled, 'Who told you about it?' Then, at some length I told him other things. 'One man played a great part in your life, and his name is Rossi.' At this point the guest elbowed the man next to him and said to me, 'Tell me more about Rossi!' But I said it had better be left alone. All at once, I jokingly added, 'What's the matter with you? Do you collect snuff boxes? You even have one full of diamonds.' He answered, 'But I didn't buy it. Someone gave it to me as a present.' All at once something else came to my mind, 'I know there is nothing wrong with it, but you have some trouble with a stiletto, why don't you give it up and be done with it?' At this, the guest jumped up and said, 'Why should I give up the stiletto? I bought it in good faith!' It developed that the Italian government claimed that the stiletto was once owned by Garibaldi and that it had been stolen. Everyone was surprised at what I said, but, in fact, the most surprised person there was myself! How is this done?"

LIVE DANGEROUSLY

"In all my lifetime I have never been attacked or harmed in any way by man or beast. Usually, when walking the New York streets, I have a feeling of harmony. But at times I suddenly get a presentiment and sense danger. Then I step aside and walk away from the area that felt unpleasant. Later, I often noted a flower pot or something crash where I was standing. I would cross the streets or zigzag when I felt the presence of something unfriendly or of a thief close by. At first, my wife thought that this was strange, but since we were never bothered and she had experienced several close calls with falling objects after I had changed our direction, she developed a sound respect for this faculty."

EVANGELINE ADAMS

"You can gain knowledge from the things you dislike if you only try to understand why you dislike them. Evangeline Adams, the astrologer, and I were friends forty to fifty years ago. She had respect for my understanding and explanation of many things in life, although I did not believe in any of her astrology. She liked my philosophy and every fourth Thursday she would have some of her friends and me over to her home. We would talk about philosophy and various matters.

"A young lady, who came quite often, approached me once and said, 'Mr. Romano, I have a friend who lives at the Savoy Plaza. She has heard a lot about you and she is anxious to meet you. She told me, "If I could only meet Jacques Romano and talk to him, he could help me a great deal." '

"I told the woman I would be happy to see her friend. She asked, 'May I bring her next time?' 'Why, certainly. I would be delighted.'

"She brought her friend to me. We shook hands, and then this woman proceeded to ignore me in such an obvious manner that everyone noticed it. I wondered, 'Perhaps she does not like me; my personality doesn't appeal to her.' Others noticed it too and, when I caught their eye, they bit their lips as much as to say, 'Look at the fool!' But I said to myself, 'I'll have to find out why she has taken a dislike to me. There must be a reason for it.' So, while she was sitting down, I passed her and stared at her hands. She looked up and seemed to be thinking. Finally, I said, 'I beg your pardon, I was in India and studied the shape of the hands, which tell me certain things. Your hands are very interesting. Would you like me to look at your hands for a minute?' She offered me her hand. I took it, turned it around, examined the fingers, —'Hmm, very interesting! Thank you very much.' I walked away, but then I could not get rid of her. 'Mr. Romano, what did you see?' 'Come over to the corner,' I said, 'over here, and I'll tell you.'

" 'Weren't you engaged to a Frenchman when you were in France recently?' 'Well, yes.' 'And it was announced in the papers that you were going to be married and wanted to come to the United States with him. There was something about the Bolsheviks having destroyed his property, and that he told you that in a short time he would gain back his losses and be all right again?' 'Yes.' 'Well, I'm going to tell you something. That fellow was an imposter. He was really a penniless Belgian, a gigolo, who posed as a Count and told you things that no one could disprove, but then, as you were making plans, you finally found out.' The woman interrupted, 'How did you know all this?' 'Very simple! Do you know why you took a dislike to me? Because I resemble that Belgian gigolo.' 'My God, will you excuse me!' "

Being a shrewd observer helps. Knowing how to describe an unusual event even though there is no satisfactory explanation is a beginning. The following episodes are intriguing, particularly because Jacques Romano was the witness.

DERVISHES IN THE SUDAN

"The Dervishes become numb and insensitive to pain in parts of their body by vigorously twirling their bodies in their ecstatic religious dances. When they are dizzy and completely intoxicated in their frenzy, they can drive an iron spike into their skulls so firmly that it takes a hammer to knock it out. You can see the spike wedged in the bone; yet there is no bleeding."

INDIA: BURIED ALIVE

"The 'being buried alive' trick is based on two things. The holy men learn how to breathe with a minimal amount of effort. I have timed some of them who can get along with only four breaths per minute. And then I noticed that when the swami was in a cataleptic state and dirt was shoveled over him, he had a tube close to his mouth, with the other end of the tube attached to a shanty many feet away, from which he got his air. Some of their feats are genuine, but more often all, or part of, their stunts are trickery."

THE FAKIR WITH AN UNUSUAL MEMORY

"When I was in India many years ago, before coming to the United States, I once saw a fakir sitting with his legs crossed and hands folded. He was begging for alms. An Englishman asked us, 'Would you like to see a really strange phenomenon?' He then took a piece of paper and told twenty of us who were onlookers to each write a word in various languages. Some used Latin, Italian, French, or other language. I used an Arabic word meaning 'revolting.' The Englishman then quickly read aloud the twenty words. Although the words had no connection with each other, and were of different languages, the fakir repeated them all correctly."

SELF-MUTILATION

"Years ago, I saw another famous stunt of the fakirs. One of them cut his abdomen open and took his intestines out. He did it like this: Every day over a year, the fakir made a small cut in his abdomen until he finally had an opening about three inches long. The fakirs were very thin, their flesh was lean, and they had no gas in their intestines. When the fakir exhibited himself to an audience, he covered himself with a white tunic and pretended to cut into the already existing opening with a dull knife. He then pulled his intestines out for a short period of time. If he is very careful he can do this for many years. As a related incident of sixty-seven years ago, I saw two Italians fighting in a saloon on Mulberry Street in New York City. One was knifed and his intestines came out. I can still recall him sitting there holding his intestines in, while drinking beer and waiting for the ambulance to come. That made me reflect upon the earlier experience with the fakir."

BLACK MAGIC

"I was dressed as a native and stood in the background. This was to be an example of mob hypnosis, using five to six hundred people at one time. I found that two things were essential. One, a monotone drum, and another a rhythmical rolling of the head to the eerie sound. The religious leader was in the middle. Scattered among the crowd, I noted, the leader had a disciple for every fifty people or so. They got the people whipped into such a frenzy that they could not stop. I then saw the leader take a naked young boy. As the crowd got more excited, he cut the boy's arm off; and then he took the arm and showed it to the people. He cut off the other arm and showed everybody. He put a white cloth over the boy, pulled it back, and again the boy was whole. Whatever the leader wanted them to see they saw. This trick, done in desolate places in India, had the same basis as the famous rope trick and was quite similar to what the magicians did in their illusions of having a box float or sawing a woman in half. The Hindus are very adept at mob hypnosis. A similar experience of mine occurred once when I was speaking to a church group. I threw my cane on the floor and through mob hypnosis convinced them that it had become a serpent. They ran for cover until I dispelled the illusion."

IMMUNITY TO FIRE

"Holy men and fanatics walk across hot coals by kicking their heels up so that their feet will quickly cool. They must have no moisture on their soles. Hindu fakirs drop a coin in molten lead and then quickly extract the coin. I have done this myself. The secret is to be completely calm and confident and again have no moisture so that the fingers will not sizzle. The melting point of lead is low."

KUDA BUX

"I met Kuda Bux in England, and he wanted me to manage him. I remember his giving a demonstration at Oxford when he walked through the fire. Some Oxford students tried it and were so severely burned that they needed extensive treatment. Years later, in midtown New York, I watched him walk through a pit, approximately fifteen yards long, and the depth was above his ankles. I could not stand the heat within three feet of the pit. In the middle of the feat he stopped and stepped up on a stone for a second while the press photographers took pictures. I was the only one he knew in the United States. Before he did his fire walk, he scrupulously followed a rigid diet. (He told me that his fire walk depended on his diet and emotional state of mind. He abstained entirely from meat. If someone dropped some meat into the pit, he knew he would be burned.)"

*   *   *

The following examples of Romano's uncanny skill were generously supplied by three distinguished persons, who knew him for many years. Besides their intrinsic value the examples indirectly tend to confirm many of the other unusual situations that are not so well documented. In the process of compiling many of these amazing episodes, it was evident that people would often acknowledge the truth of their experiences with Romano only if their names were not used. They seemed concerned that they might be publicly associated with such a man; yet in private many never hesitated to take full advantage of his extraordinary talents.

THE TELEPATHIC CHALLENGE

The following letter epitomizes much of Jacques Romano's personality and his unusual control over extrasensory perception. Harris Hammond was a friend for many years.

"The following is an account of an incident that took place at my parents' home in Gloucester, Massachusetts, where my wife and I were spending part of the summer vacation. In addition to the family gathering, father and mother had as a guest a well-known writer whom we will call Mr. X.

"One afternoon Jacques Romano telephoned from Boston to talk with me. On hearing that Jacques was in Boston, the family insisted he come to Gloucester.

"After dinner the family, who had been entertained often before by Jacques, asked him if he would do some of his sleight-of-hand card tricks, etc. This Jacques did in his own inimitable manner. Mr. X, unable to explain the baffling things that Jacques did, seemed to resent this inability on his part and became antagonistic. This attitude was expressed by his constant statements that what Jacques was doing was nothing but tricks and that Jacques's statement that he suggested certain cards to the individuals selecting them, or that he could read their minds when he asked them to think of a card, was just nonsense. Jacques replied that possibly Mr. X was right, but he would like to try an experiment with Mr. X. The success or failure of this experiment would depend entirely on Jacques's ability and Mr. X's honest cooperation. Jacques explained that in this test he required Mr. X to concentrate and picture in his mind some friend who had died. Then he, Jacques, would see what impression he could get of the individual selected by Mr. X. This was agreed upon, and Mr. X put his hands over his eyes for better concentration.

"Jacques walked slowly up and down for some seconds and then said to Mr. X, 'I am afraid you have two people in your mind. One is an elderly lady, and the other seems to be a man, so please concentrate on one or the other.' Mr. X nodded that this had been the case. After two or three minutes, Jacques said 'I am beginning to get a picture.' After another pause he said, 'I see a man . . . he is tall—he is very tall . . . he must be six feet four . . . he is wearing a white suit, and it seems too big for him in spite of his size . . . he is very tanned . . . he is in the tropics . . . I think he is British . . . he is pointing at his chin. I see nothing . . . yes, he is still pointing and I see a small scar. He is nodding . . . now he is gone.'

"Mr. X removed his hand from his eyes and leaned forward in his chair. His expression was one of complete astonishment. He said 'This is incredible. The man I had in mind was a British Consul in the Indies. He was six feet four, and it was a standing joke that even with his size he always wore his white tropical uniform sizes too large for him. The most amazing thing—while I was staying with him he cut his chin while shaving. The cut was quite small but some infection followed that caused his death.'

"A thing to note is that all during this description by Jacques, Mr. X had his hands over his eyes and never indicated by expression or word whether Jacques was right or wrong until Jacques finished.

"To the question by Mr. X as to whether Jacques thought it was the Consul's spirit he saw or a mental picture of Mr. X's Jacques replied that all he could say was he had a vivid mental picture of the things he had described."

Very truly yours,
(signed)   Harris Hammond

THE SORCERER'S APPRENTICE

It was 1904, and Jacques Romano was waiting in the photographer's studio when a young boy of fourteen knocked on the door and entered. When this poor delivery boy was two years old, his father had died, and now he had had to leave school after the eighth grade in order to contribute to the support of his struggling family. Romano noticed the sad-eyed young fellow and, in a gesture of friendly interest, asked him if he believed in reading palms. Romano offered to read the boy's palm. He mentioned several specific items.

"He told me what was going to happen. He told me the year that I would get married and how, shortly after, I would be divorced. Then he mentioned the exact year that I would be happily remarried the second time. He said I would not be successful until I was forty, that I would go to college and study medicine, and that I would become famous in the medical uses of electricity. I was interested enough to be silent, but I felt relieved when the photographer came out of the dark room so I could finish delivering my package. The whole incident never meant much and was blotted out of my memory until years later when I had trouble with my first wife. Then I remembered this event of long ago and was rather comforted with the thought. It also happened that when I was twenty-six I became interested in medicine, because I had accompanied my sister to the Mayo Clinic, where she was operated on by Dr. Will Mayo. At this age, I went to high school and later on undertook medical training. My second marriage occurred when predicted and was very happy. I trained abroad, and, upon my return to America, specialized in ear, nose, throat, and plastic surgery, but I gradually became more interested in the use of ultra-short waves in the treatment of disease.

"Through the years, I was a good friend of Mr. Joe Dombroff, President of Willoughby's. As time went on, we used to go fishing together at Virginia Beach. On our trips, we exchanged stories and discussed various things. One day I told him I had the weirdest experience as a young boy, when someone had told me all the things that were to happen to me. I told him how that man of long ago had predicted the exact years of my marriages, my going to medical school, my not being successful until forty, and then my eventual interest in the medical uses of electricity. This experience of long ago greatly impressed me, for at the time not much was known about the uses of electricity in medicine, and everything this man had said about me, a poor orphan boy, was very unlikely.

"Joe Dombroff pricked up his ears, 'Would you remember the fellow's name who told you this?' I said I did not think I could, but I would never forget him otherwise. Joe then told me of a committee that he, another man, and one Jacques Romano were on, and how they met with Sir Arthur Conan Doyle and showed the latter how spirit pictures could be faked. Joe said they used photographic plates that were previously exposed and then carefully rewrapped, sealed, and put in boxes until taking the phony pictures. Joe looked up at me and said, 'You know, I think I know who the man was, and I'm going to bring him around and have him meet you.' This meeting took place at 88 Central Park West, in the 1930's; and, sure enough, it was the same man of long ago, Jacques Romano."

The last part of the prophecy was fulfilled in the most extraordinary manner. When interviewed, at seventy years of age, Dr. Abraham G. Ginsberg was a slightly stooped man, with wavy white hair, thick, dark eyebrows, sad eyes, a kindly facial expression, and a soft voice. He was modest to a fault and very matter-of-fact in his manner, but the medical archives verify that he was the first man in the United States to make and then describe, in a scientific publication (*Medical Record*, December 19, 1934), an ultra-short-wave radio apparatus.

Through the years until his death in 1962, Dr. Ginsberg continued his pioneering researches. In 1934, he felt that the results obtained with ultra-short radio waves were not solely to be attributed to the heat generated in the tissues, but to a relatively heat-free effect of the radio waves. Consequently, with the help of Arthur Milinowski, a physicist, Dr. Ginsberg invented a special machine that could produce such radio waves. His apparatus was similar to radar and, at his instigation, had been used in some startling experiments by Dr. John Heller of The New England Institute for Medical Research. Dr. Ginsberg's many experiments, Dr. Heller's investigations, and the work of other scientists, as published in a leading article in the *New York Times* (Monday, April 6, 1959), offer much promise for very important advances in the understanding and treatment of many diseases.

Dr. Ginsberg at seventy was more active than ever as a master of the science and art of healing and also as an innovator in his highly original researches. He was also the only physician in the United States to win an Army-Navy "E" for his wartime electronic contributions and inventions. His works and opinions were solicited by the leading scientific institutions in the United States. He was that man who, as a fourteen-year-old orphan boy, was told by Jacques Romano, "Some day you will become famous in the medical use of electricity."

EXPERIMENT IN ASTRAL TRAVELING

Among Romano's many exploits, the following experience was recalled by Leslie S. Egbert, who was Executive Vice President of the Columbia-Minerva Corporation in New York City. In 1945 Egbert had his play, *The Boy Who Lived Twice,* on Broadway and he renewed his friendship with Romano, who helped him with some hypnotism scenes.

"Back in the early 1930's I became much interested in all forms of psychic phenomena, including extrasensory perception.

"The gentleman who involved me in much of my research was Francis Fast, a close friend and a well-known businessman, a person of great integrity. It was he who arranged one of the most startling experiences I was ever to undergo.

"It happened at a small stag party in New York City. I knew several of the guests but some were strangers to me. However, all were responsible citizens and I believe entirely ethical.

"One of the guests consented to be hypnotized and almost immediately fell into a deep trance. The hypnotist then stated that he would like to try an experiment in astral traveling and would endeavor to send his subject's intelligence on a trip. He asked for a volunteer from the group to suggest where the subject should go—'but it must be to a place no one else in the room is familiar with.'

"One of the gentlemen volunteered and a most interesting performance took place. Many years have passed and, while my memory is a bit hazy as to details, the session went somewhat as follows:

VOLUNTEER: 'Ask him to go to the railroad station in ———, South Carolina.'

HYPNOTIST (to subject): 'Go to the railroad station at ———, South Carolina and tell us what you see.'

SUBJECT (unhesitatingly): 'Rough, red brick platform— old frame station—painted red.'

HYPNOTIST: 'Good! Do you see any people about?'
SUBJECT: 'No.'
VOLUNTEER: 'Tell him to go one block south and one block west.'
               (Subject was completely oblivious to all sounds except the voice of the hypnotist)
HYPNOTIST: 'Go one block south and one block west and tell us what you see.'
SUBJECT: 'Red brick house, white picket fence—a light in the window.'
HYPNOTIST: 'Look in the window and tell us what you see.'
SUBJECT: 'Victorian room—lady.'
HYPNOTIST: 'Describe the lady.'
SUBJECT: 'Small—white hair—glasses—black dress—white collar.'
HYPNOTIST: 'What is she doing?'
SUBJECT: 'Reading.'
HYPNOTIST: 'Where?'
SUBJECT: 'Beside round table—center of room—lamp on table.'
HYPNOTIST: 'Go inside and tell us what she is reading.'
SUBJECT: 'Book called———.'
HYPNOTIST: 'What page?'
SUBJECT: (Gave number)
HYPNOTIST: 'That's fine. Now I'm going to bring you back.'

"The subject awakened and apparently had difficulty in believing he had been in a trance at all. The gentleman who had volunteered to help in the experiment was very excited and swore that all descriptions had been absolutely accurate.

"This had been very interesting, but of course so far

not really evidential, as no one in the room, except the volunteer, knew whether or not what we had heard was fact or fiction. Certainly *no one* knew what was actually taking place in South Carolina.

"During the rather animated discussion that followed, the hypnotist asked if it were possible to telephone South Carolina and verify the subject's information.

"This was promptly done, for the volunteer contacted his mother and asked her what she was doing. She replied that she was reading, but wanted to know what was wrong that he was calling her at that time of night (11:00 P.M.).

"The gentleman assured her that everything was fine but insisted that she tell him what she was reading. She replied that the book was————(the same as stated by the subject). The hypnotist then reminded him to ask the page number. When the volunteer asked her that, she was certain he was deep in his cups and said so. However, upon his insistence she went back to the book and gave us the page number. It was several pages beyond that given us by the subject—just about the number she would have covered while the call was being put through.

"The whole procedure had a sobering effect upon all of us. Until that time I had been skeptical about the authenticity of many of the things I had seen and heard, but this experience was hard to explain in any logical manner other than what it seemed to be.

"I did not know either the subject or the volunteer, personally, but the fact that they were well known by my friend, Mr. Fast, and their integrity vouched for by him, rather precluded the suspicion that the whole performance had been an act. I, personally, was convinced that I had witnessed a mysterious and wonderful phenomenon. The hypnotist and I became friends. His name was Jacques Romano."

XII

WORKING WONDERS WITH CARDS

"I asked Dr. Romano if he ever gambled. 'Not on your life,' he said."

—FROM A LONDON NEWSPAPER, FEBRUARY 2, 1936

HOUDINI, Dunninger, and Leipzig were accomplished card manipulators but, according to Dr. Wanderman, who knew them all, these three experts marveled at Jacques Romano's card feats. The card examples are described as they were seen—or as they were thought to be seen. The reader who is good at cards might like to try some of these stunts. First, however, here are some examples showing Romano's unique dexterity.

E. Swift Newton, a lifetime friend of Romano's, reported that in Jacques's prime, in the 1930's, he received an average of five invitations for dinner every night, though his name was not in the telephone book. When Newton visited Romano in his New York apartment, he often had to wait while Romano was finishing a private conference with an auto magnate, or a stock market tycoon, a theatrical celebrity, or a distinguished scientist. Jacques's wife Molly once good-naturedly remarked that when she married Jacques she knew she was getting an unusual man, "but I did not know about all this work with the cards!"

In the early 1930's, Newton was telling a friend, Philadelphia chemist Phil Sharpless, about Jacques's extraordinary and versatile abilities. Sharpless interrupted the lengthy recital with the sarcastic question, "Does this Romano also own a chain of nightclubs in New York?" However, justice was rendered to the man whom Newton called the most gentle, kind, sympathetic, understanding man of integrity he had ever met. At a party Newton gave in a huge oak-beamed high-ceilinged barn, he gave Romano a new deck of cards and said, "I would like you to go over and see that man in the corner and show him something. He has been giving me a hard time!" Romano gave Sharpless an unopened, new deck of cards, which he examined and returned to Romano, who told him to think of a card. Romano then said, "Are you sure?" He took the deck in his hands and threw all fifty-two cards to the ceiling. All the cards fell except one which stuck on a beam—the exact card Sharpless had chosen.

In recalling this incident, Romano commented that the genuine telepathic parts of his stunts which he, himself, was unable to explain were frequently overlooked by people and that it was always ironic when they seemed to become more excited about the sleight-of-hand part that any good magician could duplicate.

HOUDINI AND MYSTERIOSO

"Houdini was a first-class showman and magician. He did not believe in mind reading and spiritualism. He thought that I did my work through intuitive presentiments, but he could not explain it further.

"Another favorite stunt that I did in my prime was to talk to the audience for a while until I found in the group a very suggestible subject. I would then leave the room after instructing this subject to write a short question on the back of his calling card, put it in an envelope, and seal it. When I returned, I held the card to my forehead and then, letter by letter and word by word, I often succeeded in getting the exact question. Although the subject did not know it, I had telepathically suggested the question that he used. Like Houdini, I was baffled and could not explain how I did it myself!"

GAMBLING

"I don't have to do crooked work in cards because I can (telepathically) make someone play the wrong card every time. Once I was talking to a woman's club and stated that I never gambled or bet. One woman, who was quite a philosopher, said to another woman, 'Look at him. He's too honest. I don't think he's the type of man ever to gamble or take advantage of anybody. He wouldn't, because he has too much self-respect.' Now, what was her explanation? It is this. At heart I was a crook, but I denied myself the pleasure of being a thief."

"The eyes and mouth are made to deceive; they seldom tell the truth."

"I am so immune to false ideas and lies that it does not bother me. I say and do things, and I don't know why. Anything with merit or truth in it, I sense."

POWER OF THE LITTLE SPANIARD

"In Montgomery, Alabama, I met a salesman and asked him if he'd like to go out and eat, but he said he had no money. So, as was my custom, we went to a gambling house, where I played just long enough to win a few dollars. This was repeated for several days. The card sharks were quite baffled. When I came the fourth day they requested me to leave and go to another house. The manager asked what kind of man I was, anyway, so I picked up the $3 in silver and threw it on the floor. Later I discovered that these gamblers sent out notices to many of the houses in the South saying, 'Beware of the little Spaniard who always wins a few dollars and then quits. Find out his system!'

"In 1937 I won 10,000 francs at Monte Carlo for Prince Edward de Bourbon, the Uncle of King Alfonso. He put his arms around me and said 'Paisano.' The crowd said, 'Look at the little Spaniard who wins every time he wants to!' I would suggest to the gamblers and they would play the wrong card."

For sixty-five years, one of Romano's most popular "magic" tricks used ordinary cigarette paper as a prop. This trick has defied duplication by many famous magicians. Here is how it went.

The lady takes a piece of cigarette paper, tears it in half, and then tears one of the divided halves into many smaller pieces, which are crumpled and put in the center of the remaining intact half and rolled up into a tight little ball. She holds the ball between her thumb and forefinger. The gentleman takes a piece of paper, folds it in half, and then again in quarters. He tears the corner, so that the paper, when open, will have a hole in the center. He puts the tiny torn piece on his knee and rolls the larger remaining piece into a ball which he holds between his thumb and forefinger. Both the lady and gentleman hold their outstretched hands up while Romano gazes at them benevolently. Presto! They each unwrap their pieces of paper. The cigarette papers are switched! The torn middle piece perfectly matches! The audience is bewitched!

* * *

MY EXPERIMENTS

The following experiments were undertaken on twenty-seven different dates between Romano's ninety-second and ninety-sixth year. Ninety-three different people, males and females, between the ages of fifteen and eighty participated. Usually we gathered in my office, but sometimes we met in three other physicians' offices, a large research electronics laboratory, and three private homes. Two of the medical offices had rooms with lead-lined walls and doors such as are used for X-ray work; yet the results were substantially the same.

Because Romano's accounts of his spontaneous telepathic events appeared to involve many subtle emotional factors, the experiments were not performed under such stereotyped conditions that might inhibit the phenomena in question. Everything was done to fit in with Romano's particular mood, not to harass him, force him, or in any way compromise his unique, passive, trancelike state. During the course of the session Romano would gradually work himself into a mild frenzy or state of dissociation by talking about his many life experiences for an hour or more before proceeding with the phenomena with the cards and "spirit readings."

None of the participants interrupted Romano, and he gradually gained their rapt attention. He talked of past events (described in this work) and discussed parables as well as many original jokes and humorous situations. Nothing in the setting could be construed as routine or premeditated. None of the participants had ever met Romano before, and he knew nothing about them. Nor did the observing physicians know anything personal about the guests. Before the session many of the participants were understandably doubtful about what might happen; others were convinced that everything would be trickery and readily explainable; still others had an open mind.

The emotional attitude of Romano's audience could be described as "I know he is a liar, but I can't prove it." Most of the participants, however, were friendly in their attitude and willingly and generously lent themselves to these experiments. Most were physicians and their wives, but there were also some businessmen, lawyers, engineers, clergymen, carpenters, tailors, nurses, secretaries, waitresses, and adolescents. When the studies were undertaken in the evening, the room was well illuminated. Either unmarked, brand new, or personal playing cards that Romano had never seen before were used.

It was impossible to predict before the session what particular stunts with the cards Romano would attempt and with whom. Romano tended to divide his time between the various subjects and gave no indication of singling out anyone. At the end of all the sessions, a detailed inspection of the cards chosen revealed that all the cards were used, even including the joker, with equal frequency.

Romano often claimed that he did not know what particular stunt he would do next, or how he really accomplished these feats. He dismissed it as "I have a faculty for suggesting the cards to them, but I have to feel in the mood." By that he meant having the card in mind himself, and then by suggestion (telepathic means?) implanting that card in the participant's mind. However, this could explain only some of the stunts. When people tried to trip him up, he would mention the alternative card they had in mind. At such times it appeared as though he were receiving their thoughts. In many instances, the participants wrote on a slip of paper what they perceived or thought they had seen, or they shared their information with the person sitting next to them, so that when the feat was over they could not claim that they were hypnotized in some strange way and then had the answer suggested to them.

Aside from the intrinsic control against conscious or unconscious deception provided by the nature of the feats described below, there was also a further biological control. The functional status of Romano's hearing and vision would seem to rule out any means of perceiving by these channels. He was unable to hear a ticking watch placed alongside the openings of his ears, and he could just barely hear a whispered voice at the same location. Because of his telepathic abilities, special precautions were taken in checking his vision. For instance, an eye chart had to be used that was unfamiliar to the eye specialist. Since this physician, who was a Professor of Eye Disease at a New York medical school, used the standard eye charts in his work, he would have unconsciously memorized the eye chart. Thus there was the risk of Romano "reading" the eye specialist's memory, rather than perceiving with his (Romano's) eyes the chart placed before him. With the glasses Romano used for correcting his nearsightedness in everyday activities, he was able to read, at a distance of ten feet, letters that if his vision were normal he should have read correctly at forty feet (10/40). However, his near vision revealed no defects since he could read, under good light, the finest print on a test chart.

Special tests were then devised using the playing cards in such a way as to simulate the experiments. Though Romano could detect the color black at six feet, and the color red at four feet, he could not correctly distinguish the specific features of one card from another at these distances. Romano's only other eye changes presumably affecting his visual accuracy consisted of early opacities in both lenses. It was therefore concluded that, if Romano were to perceive the cards via sight or hearing, he would have had to have considerably better eyesight and hearing than he apparently possessed. Unfortunately it was not possible to test him with a blind person and a deaf mute. In these two separate cases, the specific disabilities might tend to rule out Romano's suggesting to them a specific card by means of seeing or hearing as might occur with people of unimpaired vision and hearing.

CARD SELECTION

For this feat a deck of cards was shuffled and then fanned out in Romano's hand before the subject's eyes so that Romano saw only the backs of the cards. The subject was told to look at the cards and then keep one in mind. The deck was put back together and Romano told the subject the card. He did this correctly on sixty-six occasions and failed ten times. He was equally successful with three patients who had disruption of healthy brain function. One had had a lobotomy operation for his still-existing psychosis, one had had massive destruction of the right frontal lobe, and a third, widespread brain changes resulting from an automobile accident.

The subject took a card out of a shuffled deck, looked at it, reinserted the card in the deck, and then reshuffled it. Romano took the deck in his hands and then correctly selected the card the subject had chosen. As a variation, Romano would hold the deck in his hands, behind his back, and then correctly choose the card. He performed the feat and its modifications, without error, one hundred and thirty-three times, with ten failures. He was equally successful with the patients with frontal lobe brain damage.

THINK OF A CARD

Romano asked his subject to think of a card, which Romano then identified for color, suit, digit, or picture. He succeeded sixty-four times and failed sixty-nine times. His results with the three brain-damaged patients were essentially similar to those with other patients. He often correctly named the card on the second or third trial. He also often correctly told the subjects the card they had originally chosen before they changed to another card.

Once this stunt was attempted during a brain-wave recording. Initially, Romano had three consecutive failures with one subject. The subject evidenced tension and lack of understanding. But Romano then succeeded with the

Jack of Diamonds, after which there were three more failures. He turned his attention to a second subject with whom he had previously been very successful in telling her things about her past life. Again he had three failures. But then, in quick order, he had one success, one failure, and three consecutive successes. In all, with the two subjects while Romano was having a brain wave recorded, he had five successes out of twelve trials. During this time there was no grossly discernible change in the brain wave pattern. However, this does not rule out the possibility that more refined techniques, such as having wires inserted deeply into various areas of the brain, might have yielded some clues.

THINK OF A CARD—TELEPHONE

This feat was the same as "Think of a Card," but done over the telephone. Romano was successful five times and failed once.

"TRUE HALLUCINATION"

One subject selected a card from a freshly shuffled deck and, without looking, placed it face down on his body. Romano fanned out the remaining cards before a second subject's eyes. This subject then mentally selected a card and stated his choice aloud. But when he examined the deck, he failed to find his card, although he often vehemently insisted it must be there. The first subject then looked at the card he had originally selected and placed on his lap. This was the one that was "seen" by the second subject. Of twenty-four trials Romano had twenty successes and four failures. One of the successes occurred with the patient who had extensive frontal lobe damage.

NAMING THE CARD NO ONE SAW

Romano shuffled a deck of cards and then a subject cut the deck. The top card of the cut deck was removed and placed face down under an opaque object—an ashtray, for instance. The cut deck was then put back together by the subject. Some distance away, Romano then named the card under the opaque object. He was correct seventeen times and failed once.

TWO-DECK FORCED SHUFFLE

One subject shuffled and cut a deck of cards. The procedure was duplicated by a second subject with another deck of cards. The top cards of the cut deck were examined by each subject independently. On fifteen occasions both subjects came up with the same card. There were no failures.

AMAZING TWO-DECK FEAT

Romano fanned one deck of cards before the eyes of the subject, who selected a specific card. A second subject shuffled another deck and cut. The top card of the cut remainder of the deck was examined. In thirty-four trials

Romano had correctly "matched" the cards thirty-one times and failed three times.

Another variation of this feat was to have one subject look at another subject and think of the card. The second subject shuffled a deck and cut to the card thought of by the first subject. This was done correctly three times. A second variation was this: Romano spread a shuffled deck face down on a table, a subject "randomly" selected a card, looked at it, and then "randomly" returned it to the spread deck. Romano told the subject what his card was and the specific card that was immediately next to it. This was done correctly seven times. On one occasion a subject pulled a card and shuffled again while a second subject followed this same procedure with a second deck. Both subjects exchanged their decks and searched for the card they had originally chosen. When the cards were examined they were both the Queen of Hearts.

*   *   *

In evaluating the card feats one must avoid drawing any conclusions until the most rigid precautions and controls are established. With Romano any such control measures would have had to be designed so as not to constitute an emotional straitjacket and thus inhibit the give and take and ever-changing interpersonal nuances between the members of the audience or the specific sender-receiver and Romano.

Professor J. B. Rhine, the great pioneer parapsychologist, told the author how on one occasion at the Union League Club, New York City, Romano did not succeed with the cards when requisite safeguards were interposed. However, if all the 133 "Think of a Card" experiments were done consecutively and mechanically in one or two sessions, perhaps they too might have failed instead of having close to 50 per cent success. Possibly Romano's unusual degree of success in this specific test may be attributed to the imposition of safeguards that *were* more suitable to his emotional makeup. First there was a comfortable emotional rapport. He usually did only a few such "Think of a Card" feats during a single session; when the results over several years were tabulated, sixty-four successes and sixty-nine failures were noted.

In studying Romano, the scientist had to be a member of the audience, with a natural reaction of awe and amazement as he wholeheartedly entered into the spirit of the evening and joined in all the collective "ahs," sighs, and laughter. The scientist had to be the sober, vigilant, ever-watchful observer of Romano and the subject-participants. No detail of verbal comment or nonverbal behavior, such as a gesture, scratch, cough, or angry growl would be too trivial to escape his attention. As with the words and behavior of his patients, everything had meaning and significance. The scientist pondered the meaning of the failures, which were many, as the factors surrounding success. He was impressed by the frequent patterned confusion between Romano's suggestion and the percipient's false answer. That is, for example, the substitution of the structurally similar 3 for 8 or the 6 for 9, and vice versa. Then, in the sphere of similar sounds the 2 is often confused with the 10 and the ace for the 8 and vice versa. Also, as admitted by the baffled subject-participants in many of the card experiments, the card they thought of or looked at was frequently the correct card chosen before they "changed their minds" to a second card which they gave as an answer. As can be seen, parapsychological successes are often factual errors. It was usually the fleeting, quickly changing, percept that was transmitted and perceived by Romano and subject-participants. In no instance did a subject-participant become aware that the cards he thought of or that he looked at were not really his own choice but actually (telepathically?) suggested to him by Romano.

What a person claims to be true need not necessarily be accepted as a fact. As Romano said, there is your side to the argument, his opinion, and the facts. One's experiences with another person, over a long period of time, tend to provide evidence about that person's character, honesty, and ways of describing reality. Thus, Romano stated that the "Think of a Card" feats were not mixed with sleight-of-hand. He admitted, however, that the other stunts were probably a combination of factors, although he himself often did not know when it was genuine extrasensory perception or a mixture. That a problem exists and that its relevant data cannot be satisfactorily explained should not mean that it is fraud. That such data are involved with complex subjective psychological experiences should not mean that they should be neglected for the sake of so-called pure laboratory objectivity and quantification. This is a problem for a parapsychologist who is also an expert card player and magician.

It is hoped that this careful description of Romano's card feats will move some readers with ability in this area to attempt to mobilize their dormant skills and develop talents akin to those of Romano. Certainly if such talents can be developed with cards, the implications would be great. With these precautions and reservations about how to interpret Romano's many card feats, attention can now be directed to a series of more provocative experiments— "spirit reading"—where Romano's information was challenging and freer of any possible taint of sleight-of-hand or suggestion.

XIII

WISDOM CONJURED FROM THE PAST

*"He does experiments in mind-reading that are above
description, explanation. You can't describe this
Jacques Romano. You see. And wonder!"*

—LECTURE POSTER (ABOUT 1943)
MANAGEMENT HAROLD R. PEAT, INC.

ALTHOUGH not a spiritualist, Romano called one of
his mind-reading telepathic abilities "spirit reading." He believed that he could obtain impressions of
thoughts and information about people who had died long
ago. He said, "If you understand your bodily and mental
state, you can get hunches and presentiments all the time,
but you only get an impression when you don't fill your
head up with a lot of irrelevant material. Your mind must
be a blank. When I do this work, I am oblivious to everything else on the face of the earth, to all sounds, sights,
and distractions. My mind must be clear. There is no
anger or anxiety. I must just want to do it. I isolate myself from the whole world."

In the middle of an evening or after he had observed
the participants' nonverbal reaction to his mono-
logue, Romano would select someone from the audience
and give him a piece of cigarette paper. Romano instructed
the subject to roll up the paper into a little ball and put
it between his opposed forefinger and thumb. The subject

held this in his outstretched hand and brought it in apposition to the point of a soft lead pencil in his other hand. Romano then said, "Think of someone you have known well for many years, someone who is dead. The longer you have known the person and the more you know about him, the more vibrations I get. Don't think of a child because he did not have enough experience in life to leave an identity. There can never be any embarrassment in what I have to say because I only speak what the whole world can know. Do not think about a soldier, because if I tell you all about the soldier and his life, three members of his family will become upset and might then go to a charlatan who can bring them too much grief. The deceased soldier's mother, his wife, and his sister would understandably confuse what I am doing.

"Now, I want you to be very quiet and listen to me. I will tell you things and recall events that you, yourself, have long since forgotten. Whatever you do, say nothing until I am finished. Do not interrupt or I cannot do it."

Romano assumed at times different postures and characteristic facial expressions of the deceased. He described many apparently significant events in their lives. The spirit reading usually lasted five to fifteen minutes. Romano seldom used a woman as a subject because he felt women were too easily overcome with emotion and often did not tell the truth about their age, and thus confused the chronology of the reading.

In eight out of fourteen spirit readings which the writer observed, Romano correctly spelled the letters and then gave the Christian names of the deceased whom the subjects were thinking of. In the other instances he got most of the letters correct but could not synthesize them into the name. For instance, he got in incorrect order all of the letters for the Norwegian name *Torger,* except the *g.* In one case, where he "failed," he correctly perceived three of the letters but was thrown off by the subject's insisting that he was wrong. The subject could not himself, it turned out, correctly spell the name *Eleanor.*

In many instances Romano provided additional first or last names of persons who were close relatives or friends of the deceased. Several times, Romano astounded his subject by telling him that he had switched from a man to a woman in thinking of a name or vice versa. If Romano began incorrectly or was interrupted, he would change the subject and, apparently, work himself up into a trancelike state again. Then after "erasing" his mind he would start over again.

A total of twenty names was given by Romano, which seemed to make sense and conform to the subjects' memories of the correct facts. Even where the names were incorrect, Romano usually provided enough pertinent information so that the subject felt he succeeded in the "spirit reading."

During the readings Romano's face would sometimes become contorted. He would take his glasses off and put them on or suddenly grasp his abdomen and gasp for breath. Sometimes he appeared depressed when describing a suicide. Once he held his chin, as if in pain, before proceeding to mention a fractured jaw sustained in an auto accident. Other widely diverse significant life experiences he described, and which were later said to be true by the participants, included "tremor of the fingers," "caught in barbed wire," "serious infection from an ingrown toenail," "motorcycle accident," "a wheelchair case for years and crippled with arthritis," "loss of a business by a recent fire" (giving the correct time of the incident), "breathing obstruction in the neck" (thyroid disease), "heart attack," "lameness resulting from a fractured hip," "chronic alcoholism," "study of foreign languages and particular interest in French," "paralyzed fifth finger from a fight in a grocery store," "mutilative leg scars," "a life intimately connected with horses" (Pony Express rider), and "decapitation in an auto accident."

In many of these instances Romano gave the approximate or exact age at onset of illness and death or the time of the event. By his acting, gesticulating, tone of voice and manner of speaking, he often so successfully imitated the deceased that the subject was amazed. In some instances the wives of the subjects cried out in astonishment.

Romano frequently "recalled" such personality traits pertaining to the deceased as "vile temper" . . . "played the piano" . . . "a busybody" . . . "very stubborn" . . . "hard" . . . "fighter" . . . "willful" . . . "sensitive" . . . "readily absorbs knowledge" . . . "envied by his associates and having a hard time for three years" . . . "an aunt wanted to adopt him" . . . "the wife needed surgery but it was put off because of fear" . . . "liked 'happy shoes' for some silly reason" . . . "wrote heavily and illegibly" . . . "a tall brother who speculated" . . . "athletically inclined" . . . "very poor in mathematics" . . . and "a policeman with very big hands."

As far as could be ascertained in the observed readings, Romano was seldom completely incorrect in his statements. Judging by the subject's verbal response and, more particularly, by his reactions of amazement, it seemed that Romano was right many times.

At the conclusion of the reading, the subject would be asked to unfold the tight ball of cigarette paper and then would find written, in pencil, the name or nickname of the deceased. Some of the subjects claimed that the signature was a good facsimile of that of the deceased. Although the subjects were astonished by this, and it was impossible to determine how it was done, there was a break in the technique at one point during the reading. Romano, seemingly in an angry mood, would then help the subject tighten his fingers on the rolled cigarette paper ball, at which time he presumably exchanged, through sleight-of-hand, the paper for the one that he had secretly written the name on. Yet this was never detected during the spirit reading, or even when checking an amateur motion picture strip.

In his honesty, Romano revealed that this part of the reading was entertainment, quite separate from the facts that he could correctly obtain: the letters and the citation of names and significant events apparently in the memory of the subject. On a few occasions Romano privately told me, earlier in the day, about the names and some specific data about the deceased. This was verified several hours later in the evening to everyone's astonishment, including Romano himself!

Once, in the early hours of the morning, after a particularly successful reading, Romano said, when everyone had gone home, "I felt like it was in the good old days. I knew I got results. There was no hesitating. I just shot it off. It came very naturally. I just do it. If anything is natural to one, why talk about it? Would I tell you that I have two legs to walk, two eyes to see? How can I talk about it and say I'm psychic when it's natural and just comes to me? That's it!"

Because of this tendency to fare better sometimes than on other occasions, it would appear to be of interest to assemble as much data as possible about Romano's past readings. Although he had been performing this feat for more than sixty years, and many friends had seen him give spirit readings countless times, surprisingly little was remembered and, unfortunately, virtually nothing recorded. The highly charged personal nature of such material is often forgotten and, of course, not willingly revealed through the mails or via the telephone to an unknown physician. Fortunately there are some exceptions.

One good friend of Romano, Leslie Kuhn, a newspaper man, remembered how Romano correctly spelled the name of a deceased, Reinhold, and then correctly described this man's death while skiing in the Swiss Alps thirty-five years earlier than the reading, which was given in 1942. Mr. Kuhn also mentioned some skeletons in the closet which Romano privately recalled for some visiting reporters. One event concerned the "shotgun" marriage of a close relative of a reporter.

A scientist who had known him well remembers how Romano had correctly told him about a friend he was thinking of, who had a "house with strange stones inside and a pointed slate roof. He bought a church!" The scientist also recalled how Romano shocked an opera singer by correctly telling him he was really a butcher. It is an interesting fact that when Romano spontaneously recalled the many past readings, they never varied in essential details from what was reported by the original subjects or witnesses at a later time.

Romano himself recalled the time when he spelled all the letters of a name that the subject had thought of; but he was unable to put them together. The deceased was the subject's grandmother and her name was Pocahontas. Romano correctly told a famous explorer that he had a narrow escape in the Orient from someone with long hair who tried to kill him. He said that the explorer had taken a shot at the assailant and had torn his chest open with the bullet, which was not an ordinary type but a dum dum bullet. Romano correctly told someone about his father, who drowned when the subject was eight. On another occasion he told a physician subject he had been kidnapped when three years of age. Although always a gentleman and discreet in what he said in public, Romano confided that on a few occasions, and then only in private, he had told people of events which were upsetting yet true. Such situations included illegitimate pregnancies, business reverses, and details of a woman's disappointing love affairs. Romano asserted that he frequently picked up information of this type, but carefully censored it.

MIND READING

In fourteen instances it was possible for me to observe and record Romano's direct readings on people he had just met for the first time. I had more than a passing acquaintance with five of these people. In one instance, Romano gave two separate readings, at different times, on the same subject and was apparently very successful. In many ways the material Romano recalled was similar to that of the "spirit readings."

He gave a reading to a young lady twice, correctly describing her boy friend, his Christian name, their breakup, her relatives in the South, her aunt's name, and her embarrassment in church when being teased by a man called Elmer. The lady was quite shocked when Romano told her of a neighbor who had recently had eye trouble. The neighbor, in fact, had lost his eye recently, and this disfigurement was upsetting to the subject. The second reading with this same person revealed similar material. This particular subject had a past history of trancelike phenomena, including sleepwalking, sleeptalking, and much daydreaming. During the two readings, brain waves (electroencephalograms) were made while Romano had his eyes closed. As with the card feats, there were no discernible changes.

Romano told a young woman her coat sleeve was recently mended, which she politely denied. But later, the next day, she corrected this by stating how, at the exact time Romano had made his statements, her mother was mending the coat sleeve. Romano told a man that he had a severe knee disease, and this gentleman later said that he had had surgery for an inflamed knee joint. There was nothing about the man's appearance or gait to suggest disability. Other significant information about various subjects included a father's serious misunderstanding with a "lazy reverend"; "a desire to be a reporter"; "a runaway horse and buggy while being rushed to the hospital"; "a failure in bookkeeping while working in a music store, which was a grave setback early in life"; a serious illness and pain in the right side and leg of a healthy-appearing young man, which was called by him "a ruptured intervertebral disc . . . the most severe illness I ever had."

One subject was told about his aptitudes in electrical engineering and architecture. These particular propensities, although not correct for the subject, were applicable to his fraternal twin. Once, after completing a reading for a man, Romano turned to the wife and said, quite emphatically, that her mother had been in very poor health in 1913 and moved to the South to recuperate. This woman had not been born at the time, and knew nothing about this. But she rushed upstairs to inquire about this information from her aged mother, who then told her that both she and her husband, the subject's father, had had pneumonia in 1913 and, as a consequence, had been forced to move to North Carolina for a prolonged convalescence!

Shortly after meeting a middle-aged contractor for the first time, Romano correctly told him he was connected with roads, and how despite his love of animals he shot a "bay horse with a black mane in 1919" because of the horse's infected leg. The contractor was an animal lover and this was a particularly distasteful memory that he never mentioned.

Once when Romano did poorly on a reading and produced material that was mostly incorrect and impossible to confirm, the subject was negatively disposed and repeatedly challenged Romano with sharp retorts. On this occasion Romano had apparently not worked himself into a trancelike, passive state and he gave incorrect names, dates of marriage, and uncertain material about past events in the subject's life. But it was a rare occasion when he couldn't "tune in" correctly.

In three instances it was possible to see if Romano was successful with people who had serious mental illness or brain defects. In one case, he told about an accident five and a half years before that had changed the subject's life. "You had a bad knock on the back and also, later, trouble with the right knee." The subject was amazed, since his brain tumor was first manifest at that time, when he had a spell of unconsciousness following a fall on his back. He also smiled about the reference to the knee, because it was a secret known to very few that he had worn lifts in his shoes for many years.

Another subject was a middle-aged man with a history of a brain lobotomy for serious mental illness. As far as could be ascertained, Romano correctly told this man the significant events leading up to his first hospitalization. The particular difficulty that Romano told about and the patient confirmed centered around a card game which had led to a fight and the subject's wife calling the police. Part of this history was checked out by the patient's hospital record and was unknown to either Romano or the author. It was impossible to determine from other sources the correctness of much of the information, which the patient asserted was factual. This consisted chiefly of some names of family members and the patient's disgust with a new pair of shoes he had received and discarded three weeks prior to the reading.

The third patient was a middle-aged woman with a chronic mental illness characterized by a state of extreme suspiciousness and delusions of persecution. Although the patient confirmed many items that Romano told her, it was again impossible to determine the degree of accuracy. There were no superficial evidences of this woman's past extremely destructive behavior, but Romano correctly told the author in private of several instances, and this was later verified in her hospital chart.

COMMENT

Certain observations and criticisms are in order with this bird's-eye view of clinical data. Of course it would

have been desirable to have many more details, either con-
firming or denying many of Romano's statements. Yet,
desirable as this is, there still exists much first-hand information which the subjects verbally confirmed or suggestively confirmed by their emotional reactions. In some
instances, Romano's statements were immediately denied,
but were afterward confirmed by the subject himself or
by a relative. This was the case with the examples of the
mended coat sleeve and a hand injury that the subject
believed to be quite insignificant but which his wife recalled as being upsetting to the subject and to the whole
household.

In another instance, Romano insisted that a man had
had trouble for years with "discomforting pain" in his
lower right abdomen. The man repeatedly denied this
until Romano mentioned the hernia. At this juncture the
subject smiled broadly and said, "Yes, you're right. Why
didn't I think of it myself? Of course!"

Almost all the material appeared to be related to areas
of emotional significance to the subject. Except for scientific purposes, it would be uncalled for, and perhaps
medically ill-advised, to obtain the facts about the associated events which were often emotionally upsetting and
potentially dangerous to the patient's health. The data
were frequently concerned with serious bodily illness, deformities, and secrets that the subject had either forgotten
or, understandably, preferred to keep to himself. Such
"brain picking" in a captive audience would appear to
depend in some measure upon their cooperation and,
since most of the subjects did not necessarily understand
the potential (unconscious) significance of the information,
the matter could not be pushed to its logical end without
careful psychiatric examination of each subject. There

was often so much disguise and distortion that, if the subject were consciously aware of all the material and could openly divulge it, there would still exist the distortions arising from personal blind spots which could only be uncovered by many hours of intensive psychiatric examination. Certainly, without all the necessary data from each subject, it would be difficult to see how the superficial or consciously reported information could be rigidly scrutinized, from a mathematical point of view. If criteria could be established, it might be wondered how all the data could be numerically appraised and then how mathematical measures could be applied to the myriad complex elaborations and distortions of the original event, and the consciously and unconsciously denied, painful, often shameful past life experiences.

Despite all the foregoing, some facts emerge from these readings. First, the material Romano produced in his nineties seemed entirely similar to the reported material and statements given about his readings throughout his earlier years. In all these instances, Romano had what would appear to be extraordinary success in recalling specific names, dates, illnesses, significant personality quirks, and experiences in the subject's past life.

Romano, the shrewd observer of reactions between people, the man without formal education, apparently developed an ability that is nonexistent or dormant in most people. Under the described conditions the errors appear insignificant when contrasted with so many startling successes. Yet, as with the incorrect cards, the "failures" should also be open to the same scrutiny as the successes. As Freud showed long ago, the telepathic event can be so disguised that, without much intensive study and knowledge of the subject participant, his unconscious mind, and mental mechanisms, it is difficult to separate the wheat from the chaff. Thus, one should not discard many so-called failures without first studying all aspects of the problem carefully to determine which might really be genuine but masked telepathic events.

It would appear that there were no outstanding qualitative differences in the spirit readings about deceased persons as consciously recalled by the subject, the readings on the personal past lives of the subjects themselves, and, finally, in a very few instances, Romano's statements about some of the past memories of patients with severe brain defects and/or mental illness. This latter factor further suggests that the particular damaged areas of the brain are not necessary for the success of the spirit reading, and that what Romano recalled came from undamaged areas. Certainly, it is farfetched to imagine that Romano himself could have had access to any of the information he evoked in these "spirit readings." For the most part the data Romano recited were known only to the subject or, in some instances, to a few other people present. A startling, and not infrequent, feature is that Romano would recall specific material about the subject that the subject was not immediately aware of or even persisted in denying at first.

With the exception of the reading with the one negatively disposed subject, Romano's success did not vary significantly from one subject to another. But Romano had to be in an agreeable mood, work himself into a trancelike passive state, have a friendly, attentive audience, and at no time be interrupted once he started. By becoming completely passive he successfully put himself in his subject's shoes and correctly obtained and synthesized impressions on significant situations in the past life of the subject that might have corresponded to similar experiences in his own life.

In his trancelike state Romano was in harmonious contact with his own unconscious. Critical, intellectual functions were held in abeyance. At such times he appeared able to exercise a degree of control over his telepathic abilities, and he communicated with the subject's unconscious, his forgotten memories, and life experiences. While in this trancelike state Romano was supremely self-confident, without self-consciousness or anxiety. If he was challenged or interrupted by a subject, the process was compromised and errors were increased. His subjects usually had either a positive, friendly attitude, in expectation of success, or a negative attitude of complete incredulity and anticipation of failure. But in both cases Romano had their rapt attention. He seemed to succeed better with subjects who had strong feelings one way or the other than with subjects who were completely indifferent.

All the "spirit and mind readings" would appear to be entirely free of deception. Considering all the material that Romano produced, in addition to the allowable element of lucky hits, circumstances, and coincidences, there still remained a hard core of mysterious "foreign body" facts completely unexplainable unless presumptively telepathic or psychic.

How did this telepathic ability work? With no direct evidence for support, it may be speculated that Romano's "vibrations" were similar to what Dr. A. J. Ginsberg said in 1934: that "every normal tissue cell has a radio frequency of its own and that when these cells become changed as a result of disease (the altering emotional state), their frequency is also changed." With his unique mental control Romano was perhaps able to detect these possible high-energy vibrations and then reinterpret them as the actual experiences or memories. Analogous to someone who was born with a musical ear, Romano went beyond this by training himself to become a virtuoso in perceiving and interpreting vibrations. Romano, the shrewd, self-confident, intuitive extrovert, learned how to develop his unique talents and to understand how telepathic perception was different from ordinary perception and how it was related to his interaction with other people. By careful, retrospective analysis of his many life experiences, Romano thus learned how to interpret these "vibrations" so successfully that his sense of reality was not compromised. Indeed, it often seemed as though he had "heard it before and was trying to recall."

In what organ might this occult function originate? All the evidence from Romano's past and the reported psychic experiments suggest a biological foundation for his ability. The human brain has two areas (the visceral brain, or rhinencephalon, and the ascending reticular substance) that are anatomically and functionally connected and which might satisfy many of the requisites for "psychic" function. One area (ascending reticular area) is chiefly concerned with the state of consciousness, wakefulness, bodily tension, or anxiety. The other area (rhinencephalon) correlates sensory perceptions from the eye, ear, nose, body wall and apertures, sexual organs, lungs, and gastrointestinal tract. It is currently felt that mental activity may be greatly dependent on the subtle balance between this correlative area, where experiences are interpreted in terms of feelings, gratification, fear, defense or attack, and the more recently acquired parts of the brain (neocortex) that are involved with verbal symbols, abstraction, intelligence, and critical thinking. With its close connection to another part of the brain (temporal lobe, where memories are stored) the old visceral brain thus serves to span the spectrum of memory. On one end of the spectrum may be found early memories of various bodily sensations where time and space are of little consequence, and at the other end one might find memories of specific highly concrete experiences.

Although such theorizing is admittedly speculative, these two areas could be well suited for the type of telepathy that Romano demonstrated. For example, his passive trancelike state (dissociated state) might serve to shut out all the extraneous stimuli and anxiety that could impair his ability to selectively (telepathically) transmit or receive vibrations from the ancient correlative part of the brain. Many of his telepathic successes may have depended on his unusual ability to interpret the "vibrations" as they are received in this phylogenetically ancient correlative area and relayed to appropriate centers having to do with visual perception (clairvoyance), perception of sounds (clair-audience), and various muscular and psychosomatic responses. These latter reactions could be illustrated by the histrionics of a spirit reading: grimaces, gestures, gesticulations, pains in the chest or abdomen, shortness of breath, "growls from the stomach," and so forth. When there was little anxiety, or the unknown physiological factors that accompanied the particular moods of Romano and the subjects were optimal, greater areas might be activated (temporal lobe) and whole memories and time-space relationships could be uncovered. The frequent findings of approximate answers and confusion of symbols could thus be ascribed to the relative repression or absence of these mitigating factors.

In sophisticated adult life, with the emphasis on the intellect, the earlier experiences of emotional responses that are sensed, empathized, and intuitively (telepathically?) felt must be pushed out of awareness or domesticated. With maturation there is the necessity for inhibiting aggressive and erotic drives. Possibly with this inhibition, telepathic function, which might be mediated by the same or closely related brain area, may also be suppressed. Therefore, the telepathy that might not be uncommon between a young child and his parents is so completely repressed and disguised that to all intents and purposes it is seldom noticeable in the adult.

Whether, therefore, telepathic function is, as some maintain, a vestigial evolutionary faculty or, as is also possible, a newly acquired function of considerable value in perceiving feelings, learning, and looking backward (and forward?) in time is not easy to decide. Romano's life would seem to indicate a successful use of this function. Rather than succumbing to a psychosis from his extraordinary life of "unreality," Romano had a healthy, constructive grasp of reality. Perhaps he accomplished this by learning how selectively to utilize telepathic function by "tuning (himself) to what is truthful (real)." For Romano telepathy saved him (and others) from grave situations on more than one occasion. It may be supposed, then, that the evolutionary interpretation—a throwback or a faculty that we are still in the process of developing— remains an open question for future research.

XIV

ROMANO'S WRITINGS: GUIDEPOSTS FOR LIVING

"Learn how to have your neighbor love you as you love yourself; it will teach you consideration for others."

IN a long lifetime of myriad experiences and various careers, Romano dabbled in many fields allied to the arts, sciences, and the occult. Possibly because of his lack of early formal education, he never put in writing many of his original and cogent views when he was in his prime. But then, as he himself said, if he had been so busy writing and formally recording his many adventures, much of the spontaneity and joy of living might have been lost and the events might never have happened. Fortunately he did write a few things which are quite typical.

In November, 1939, at age seventy-five, before a nation-wide radio audience (the Mutual Broadcasting Company), Romano described some of his philosophy of life, background, and training. The audience response was enthusiastic, and Romano answered with an open letter:

Dear Radio Friend:
Please accept my thanks for the regard you have shown me after having heard my broadcast. I cannot answer your letter personally but I have tried to make this information representative of the knowledge you desire.

My education and knowledge are based on as much intelligence as I was born with and its application to life. I have wandered with camel caravans and many of my good fellow wanderers are still camel drivers.

I do not commercialize soul or spiritual development. The progress of self-development is based on *patience* and understanding. One does not have to go to foreign lands to study. Right here in this country you can practice the Sermon on the Mount.

People are inclined to lay much stress on the place of birth and nationality, a condition which has no bearing on mental or spiritual development. I was born in this universe. The United States is my home. I am an American by choice.

The mental faculty of stopping the pulse, stopping the blood circulation in parts of my body, stopping and starting digestion, raising or lowering the blood pressure, has come with practice and has nothing to do with religious beliefs or soul development.

No true Yogi has ever come to America, and any person who writes about the life of Yogis has never met a true Yogi.

The mental and physical aspirations of many seekers have been abused by numerous self-styled teachers and money-making impostors.

To commercialize the weaknesses and heartaches of people is unpardonable.

Learn to understand with humility instead of superiority. Learn how to have your neighbor love you as you love yourself; it will teach you consideration for others.

Hate is a confession of fear and lack of self-confidence. Avoid those who spread propaganda of hate, regardless of what religion they profess or position they hold. The God-given rays of the Sun baptize all earthly creatures alike without discrimination. The true Christian does not stoop to degrade the teachings of the Master, and wallow in hate, bigotry, and bloodshed.

True development rises from our mental attitude. Self-control, self-discipline, and self-mastery are the basic purposes. Only when you have attained these can you experience the exaltation of what the Great Master meant by saying "Peace be with you."

As for *health*—my mind does not recognize the proverbial three score years and ten. My mental attitude does not permit the aging process to force itself upon me.

My assurance for good health is a life without fear, worry, or hate—and with malice toward none.

Jacques Romano

*   *   *

Another glimpse into Romano's soul—his complex, melancholy, and romantic nature—is given in three poems he wrote more than thirty years ago.

THE LAW OF COMPENSATION

We should know
The great law
That holds jurisdiction.
Of self-construction,
Of self-destruction;
   The law of reaction,
Of self-reflection;
It is always with us,
In right or wrong.
It is the law of compensation.

Always here, always there,
Always prodding, always nodding,
Never ceasing;
In waking hours and sleep,
In the light, in the dark,
No hiding place for mind or heart,
Untold sensations come to pass,
In all forms of disguise.
Joy and sadness intermingled,
Tears, laughter, and remorse,
Entwined within our life.

Happiness, false and true,
Thrills, bad and good,
Pain and sorrow
Health and sickness,
Wealth and poverty in the same day,
To be saved on the battlefield,
Or slain at your own fireside,
Forebodings of danger,
Or to be consumed by flame,
It is the body, mind, and soul.

Sensing the great law,
The law of compensation;
Like a thousand judges,

All in one;
A thousand minds
Ready to define;
It warns us as it plays
With clock precision,
And expression unchanged;
The same hand uplifting,
The same hand retarding;
It touches every fiber of the flesh;
It strikes the very soul and mind.

Always reaching out to pay
The good with greater gains,
The faulty with barriers, and helping hand
To bestow honors;
To impose disgrace,
Ecstasy of soul,
Pain of body and mind;
It is always with us,
To rise from weakness
Till eternal peace is ours,
We of the great law,
The law of compensation.

SHADES OF SUNSHINE

Your station in life,
King or slave,
Master or servant,
Rich or poor,
Priest or infidel.
It is all of our making.
Artificial in its creation,
Of Man's laws of civilization;

With all your titles,
And decorations,
With all your followers,
And power of domination,
And to all who suffer destitution,
Like the shades of sunshine,
Compensation is part of you and mine.

THE IMMORTAL KISS

With sorrow and grief
Aimlessly I wandered, and
Found myself among tombstones,
The markings of repose and peace.
I tarried among them all,
My head buried in my hands,
Seeking solace for my burdened heart
And peace for my troubled soul.
All earthly trials hung
Heavily on my mortal mind.

Fainter my heart seemed to beat;
My soul pleaded for relief;
My body for existence.
For full realization I cried;
To free the body of all pain;
To give freedom to the soul.

A hazy curtain fell upon me.
My senses became transformed.
I seemed made of nothing—the I—
An ether substance of all things.
New senses came of which I never knew;
Melody without music, balmy and soft,
The ecstasy of unknown communion,
Unknown to mortal heart was mine.
Something beckoned me—a love—
A love unknown to mortals.

Who are you, a voice within me called.
An answer came with no sound—
I—I am Death.
Mortals fear me, yet
I bring peace to all weary minds.
Come with me
And you shall have eternity.

I hesitated.
Again I heard a balmy tone:
Let my followers speak to you
Of the greater glory which no mortal knows—

Life in Death—
In Death the Eternal Peace of Life.

Sounds of silent whispers filled the air.
Followers of Death, I sighed,
Make your whispers sounds of words
That the mortal in me may commune,
For I am still of earth.

Their answer came
In melody of assuring words,
And in unison they spoke:
In death we rest and are at peace;
The infinite is our rebirth,
The heavens our resting place;
The earth our footstool.

The moon responds to our moods,
The Sun a ray of candlelight,
The stars our steppingstones,
The Milky Way our roaming place.
Eternal nature is our existence.

All seasons of the year
Within the same time.
The cold and warm is not of us—
Within the Sun there is no discomfort.
There are no barriers,
There is no height,
All depths are of the surface.
To be here without coming—
To be there without going—
Everywhere without moving.
To have everything with no desire.

There is no envy:
There is no anger.
The vile cannot see us,
The unjust cannot condemn us.
We cannot be soiled,
Nor can we be made whiter.
Nothing can wound us,
Nor can the foolish praise us.

All mortal wants
Are meaningless desires.
Hatred and love are fancies unknown.
Obstacles and fear are not ours.
We are of all things
All things are ours.
We are part of all possessions.
To give is to own.
The more we give the more we take on.

We know not of man's created Hell,
Nor Heaven made of mortal mind.
No sorrow—no pain—no vengeance.
No vicious God of man to judge.
The bad and good are part of evolution.
It is forever benediction
By the eternal law of compensation
Till space and time are ours.
It is the law of re-creation
Till our image is of God.
All truth dawned upon me.
Evolution and eternity
Made themselves known.

What mockery for man of clay
To define the law of creation,
To make rules for God
And bestow upon Him
Our image of mortal flesh.
To seek mercy and salvation
With frail piety made of fear
And standard prayers
Made of man's weakness,
Words of flattery—called strength
To stimulate Hope,
The mortal's only urge.

I cried for peace and conformation.
Unassisted I was ready
To receive the kindest kiss of all—
Death's merciful touch.
The parting of ways came to pass.
Bereft of breath, the finite of me crumbled—

Mother earth was ready
To embrace the self-same dust
Into a new existence.
How strange I felt,
The law of gravity gone.
An identity of myself hovered high,
And looking down I beheld a form
Lying peacefully among the graves,
The facial smile still warm,
The glassy eyes pleading forgiveness
For all the pain the flesh
Inflicted on the soul.

Death has shown me eternal life.
May my apparition teach tolerance and peace,
The wisdom of Death, Eternal life.

*　　*　　*

In 1954 Molly Romano was afflicted with multiple infirmities and partial invalidism. Jacques Romano was despondent over her progressive failure and one day he wrote this:

THE SNOW MAN

The Clock is made of man's time.
Some of the passing hours of the day
　　become symbolic in our gamut of life.
The noon hour passed long ago.
It meant the reduction of our mortal life.

A glorious beautiful day may end with a
　　colorful sunset.
With darkness we look forward to another
　　day to come.
With the day, good or bad—all things are
　　not of my choosing;
But adaptation makes me more agreeable.
No matter what phase of life one entertains,
It is another experience to observe that
　　which is not of oneself.

The mind must be stimulated with a desire
    to seek an understanding,
To have a constructive interest, to keep
    hope alive.
When nothing more is desired apprehension
    begins;
Self-existence becomes oppressive.

With time my Spring days pass into Summer
    and Fall.
Then, followed by a Winter mantle
    covered with snow,
The Romance of my heart will react to my
    wandering mind and enjoy the end.
The same rays of the Sun will melt the snow-man
    into eternal sleep.

*   *   *

Romano's dictum applied to himself. "Do not judge me or anyone else by yourself because of your own mental attitude." The questions raised by the facts of Romano's life explore the deepest nature of man, his interpersonal relationships, and his relationship to the great Unknown —the universe. Although there are no satisfactory explanations for a man like Jacques Romano, the painstaking collection of facts is a beginning toward understanding.

Jacques Romano, the complex little man who was born in "God's world," serves as an example of inspiring hope to all people who become discouraged by advancing years and the inevitability of the aging process. Romano, by his example, showed that some extraordinary men are still on this earth and there is much more to life than the acquiring of material possessions. Although highly unconventional, he lived the spiritual life. He dramatically showed the amazing potential of a human being and the value of self-awareness and self-mastery.

His many experiences during his long life tell the story of a man of supreme self-confidence and optimism. He was one who was endowed with great energy and vitality, who early in life learned self-discipline and the ability to gratify needs and avoid excesses in his interpersonal relationships, dietary habits, and physical expressions of the life force.

By learning to adapt to ever-changing and often dangerous conditions in relation to other people and the forces of nature, Romano developed a flexibility that could ward off anxiety, shock, and needless worry. He was a master improviser. For many people, living is comparative luxury; with Romano, living often meant just to survive. Yet he could contradict this by never taking life so seriously that he was in danger of losing his wonderful sense of humor. He was interested in people, not things. He was the master of others, the flawless observer, through mastery of himself.

Romano lived each moment in the present, for all its realities, joys, sorrows, and passions. Romano applied himself to the everyday problems of life as they arose. Sometimes he cast an occasional glance forward to the future and sometimes backward to the past. He always accepted himself. He could accept his fellow man for what he was. He saw reality without cringing. If anyone could truthfully say, "I love life," it was Jacques Romano.